CREATIVE

CODING IN

PYTHON

CREATIVE

CODING IN

PYTHON

30+

PROGRAMMING PROJECTS IN ART, GAMES, AND MORE

QUARRY

SHEENA VAIDYANATHAN

Brimming with creative inspiration, how-to projects, and useful information to enrich your everyday life, Quarto Knows is a favorite destination for those pursuing their interests and passions. Visit our site and dig deeper with our books into your area of interest: Quarto Creates, Quarto Cooks, Quarto Homes, Quarto Lives, Quarto Drives, Quarto Explores, Quarto Gifts, or Quarto Kids.

First Published in 2019 by Quarry Books, an imprint of The Quarto Group,
100 Cummings Center, Suite 265-D, Beverly, MA 01915, USA.
T (978) 282-9590 F (978) 283-2742 QuartoKnows.com

Quarry Books titles are also available at discount for retail, wholesale, promotional, and bulk purchase. For details, contact the Special Sales Manager by email at specialsales@quarto.com or by mail at The Quarto Group, Attn: Special Sales Manager, 100 Cummings Center, Suite 265-D, Beverly, MA 01915, USA.

10 9 8 7 6 5 4 3 2 1

ISBN: 978-1-63159-581-3

Digital edition published in 2019

eISBN: 978-1-63159-582-0

Library of Congress Cataloging-in-Publication Data is available

Design: Landers Miller Design
Illustration: Landers Miller Design

Printed in China

To my father,
who inspired me and made me
believe I could always do more
than I thought was possible.

CONTENTS

1

CREATE YOUR OWN CHATBOTS

2

CREATE YOUR OWN ART MASTERPIECES

PYTHON

PYTHON

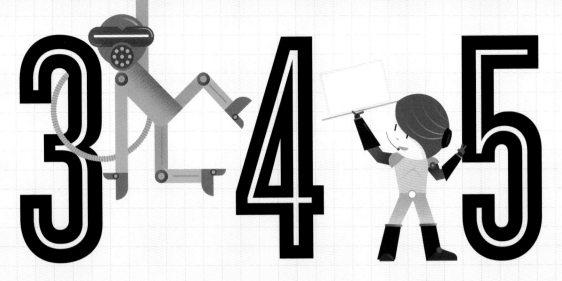

3

CREATE YOUR OWN ADVENTURE GAMES

4

CREATE YOUR OWN DICE GAMES

5

CREATE YOUR OWN APPS AND GAMES

INTRODUCTION

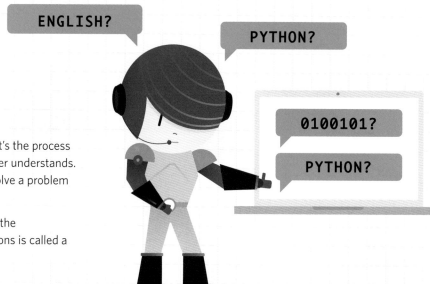

What Is Coding?

Coding is a way to tell a computer what to do. It's the process of creating instructions in a language a computer understands. Think of coding as "talking" to a computer to solve a problem or to make something, like a game or an app.

The language we use to talk to the computer is the programming language, and the set of instructions is called a **program**, or the **code**.

Why Learn to Code?

Coding is a powerful tool. It allows you to express your creativity as you make your own apps, tools, and games.

Coding allows artists and makers to create art and make wonderful objects that are only possible with code.

Learning to code helps you understand the digital world around you. The world today runs on code, from apps on a smartphone, to online shopping websites, to automated teller machines (ATMs). Because computing has had an impact on virtually every industry, understanding code will better prepare you for any kind of job.

Coding involves problem solving. Writing code requires you to break down a problem into steps, use math and logic to develop a solution, and then test and make changes to solve the problem. Learning to code engages students of all ages and helps them understand math, science, language, and more.

Why Python?

There are hundreds of computer programming languages, each with its own special purpose, as well as advantages and disadvantages. Python was created in the late 1980s by Guido van Rossum and is named after the British comedy television show *Monty Python's Flying Circus*. It has nothing to do with the snake!

Python is used to build applications on the Internet, in scientific research, and to create games, art, movies, and more. Some famous applications that have been built using Python include YouTube, Google, Instagram, and Spotify. Python is a popular language for several reasons, including:

1. It's easy to learn and use.
2. It's simple and powerful. Just a few lines of code are needed to do a task.
3. It's free and open source—which means it enjoys a massive community of users and developers who contibute to extending it to a wide variety of applications.
4. It runs anywhere, including Windows, Macs, Linux, and Raspberry Pi.

Installing Python

In order to use the Python language, you need to use a Python **interpreter** on your computer. The interpreter reads, understands, and runs the Python code. You also need a tool with which you can type and save your code.

When you download Python for free from python.org, you will get IDLE (Integrated DeveLopment Environment), which lets you create, save, interpret, and run your code.

IDLE is an example of an offline integrated development environment (IDE) for programmers. There are also a few online versions of Python. You can use a different IDE to enter and run your Python code, but the screenshots and examples in this book will show code in the Python IDLE.

Currently, there are two major versions of Python: Python 2 and Python 3. This book uses Python 3.

HOW TO USE THIS BOOK

The Python code and pseudocode are shown in a different font from the rest of the text. Comments in the code are shown in bold. The output of a program is shown under the heading Sample Run. In places where the code does not fit in one line, a \ is used to show that it wraps.

```
this is code  # and this is a comment
when code runs really long and wraps \
into a second line look for a backslash \
at the end of a line
```

Pseudocode
this is pseudocode

```
●  ●  ●              Python 3.6.1 Shell
Python 3.7.0 (v3.7.0:1bf9cc5093, Jun 26 2018, 23:26:24)
[Clang 6.0 (clang-600.0.57)] on darwin
Type "copyright", "credits" or "license()" for more information.
>>>
```

COLORS FOR DIFFERENT PARTS OF CODE

To make coding easier, IDLE can show different parts of the code in different colors. For example, the color of "hello, world", which is a Python string, may be colored green, and the color of "print", which is a Python function, may be purple. These colors and fonts can be customized by the user by clicking on the IDLE settings.

The First Line of Code

Once you've installed Python IDLE, run the application. You should see the Python shell window. The window shown at left is from a Mac, but versions on other platforms will look similar. You should see the prompt:

```
>>>
```

It's ready for you to enter code.

The Python shell is a place to experiment with snippets of code because the code runs immediately. Unless you choose to save it, code in the Python shell is lost once you close IDLE. You'll use the Python shell to test and learn the Python code that's listed in the Big Ideas sections in this book. For the projects, you'll use IDLE to enter code into a file that can be saved, changed, and run multiple times.

It's traditional to start learning to program with a classic "hello, world" program. The goal is just to get the computer to put up those words on the screen. There are variations on this simple program—from adding an "!" to using uppercase—but in this book, we use one of the earliest versions of the phrase, "hello, world".

In Python, in order to print anything to the screen—that is, to have text appear on the screen—simply type in the word *print* with the text to be printed in quotation marks inside parentheses.

So to start, in the Python shell at the prompt **>>>>**, type in the following:

```
print('hello, world')
```

The code is case sensitive—it should be typed in all lowercase letters—and the text can be in either single quotes or double quotes.

The computer should reply with "hello, world." It will then return to the prompt, waiting for more. Go ahead and type in more print statements.

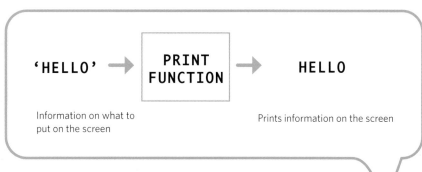

'HELLO' → PRINT FUNCTION → HELLO

Information on what to put on the screen

Prints information on the screen

Python Functions

The print code above is called a print **function** in computer programming languages. A function is code that does something. You may have seen functions in math or in a spreadsheet application (for example, the "average" function in a spreadsheet takes in a set of numbers and gives you their average). Think of Python functions as black boxes that can do something. You do not have to know how they do their magic, just how to use them. We do not need to know how print function works to put the text on the screen.

Sometimes, functions take information, and sometimes, they return information. For example, the print function takes information on what to print (the text in quotation marks) and it does just what we expect: it prints this information to the screen.

Throughout this book, we will use the word *function* instead of *command* or *code* as we introduce the Python programming language.

When you code in Python, you will be using many functions that are available in the Python language. In Chapter 4, you will learn to make your own functions.

Computers Are Picky: Understanding Errors

Type in the print code from before again, but this time make a mistake—a wrong spelling or a missing quotation mark, for example. What happens?

```
>>> print('hello, world)

SyntaxError: EOL while scanning string literal
>>> Print('hello, world')
Traceback (most recent call last):
  File "<pyshell#2>", line 1, in <module>
    Print('hello, world')
NameError: name 'Print' is not defined
>>>
```

You will see an error message in the color set by IDLE—for example, red— on the Python shell. As you can see, missing a closing quotation mark or using an uppercase P in the print command will not work.

Computers are picky! Even a small mistake in the code gives an error known as a **syntax error**. This means the language was not used exactly as it is defined; the error has to do with the syntax of the language.

Syntax errors are usually easy to fix, especially because there is either a helpful colored line next to the error or the error message explains what the computer does not understand.

Once all the syntax errors are fixed, the computer program may still not run as expected. This kind of an error is called a **runtime error**. It is due to a mistake in the way the code is being used or the way the problem is being solved. These mistakes are called **bugs** in the code. Some bugs are easy to fix, and others can take a long time. Finding and fixing these bugs is called **debugging**, and it is a critical part of learning to code.

Problem Solving:
Planning Your Code by Writing Algorithms

Learning the functions and syntax of a programming language so you can use it to give instructions to a computer is just one part of coding. The other, usually more difficult, part is to understand what instructions to give to solve a given problem.

Anytime you create something or solve a problem on the computer, you must give the computer instructions. These instructions must be defined clearly in the order in which the computer must follow them. The set of steps, in order, needed to do any task on the computer is called an **algorithm**.

We use algorithms in everyday life, though we may not call them algorithms. For example, to make a cake, we follow a recipe, a series of steps in order. That recipe is an algorithm.

To solve problems and write good code, computer programmers plan ahead by writing down the steps—the algorithm—using one of two methods: pseudocode or flowcharts.

Pseudocode

This is an algorithm written in an informal, simple natural language, such as English. It often uses indentation to organize the instructions.

For example, here is pseudocode for setting the table for four people.

Pseudocode

    Repeat 4 times the following
        Go to next empty place on table
        Put a bowl at this place
        Place a napkin to the left of the bowl
        Place a spoon to the right of the bowl

Here is pseudocode for adding ten numbers entered by the user and printing them to the screen.

Pseudocode

    Set total to 0
    Repeat 10 times the following
        Get number from user
        Add number to total
    Print the total to the screen

The instructions that are indented are repeated. In the latter example, the two indented steps—getting a number from the user and adding it to the total—are repeated 10 times. The computer then prints the total after the repetition is completed.

Flowcharts

This is an algorithm written in a visual way using a diagram of boxes and arrows to show the order of instructions. The box shapes that will be used in the flowcharts in this book are:

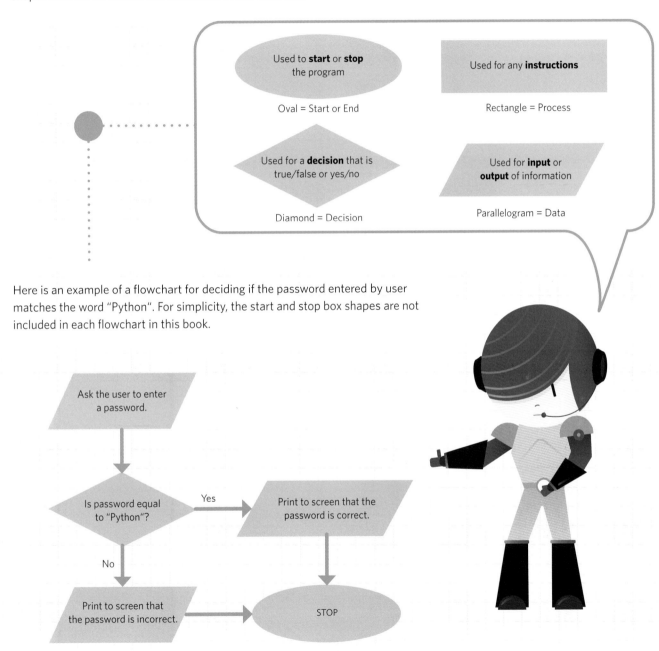

Used to **start** or **stop** the program

Oval = Start or End

Used for any **instructions**

Rectangle = Process

Used for a **decision** that is true/false or yes/no

Diamond = Decision

Used for **input** or **output** of information

Parallelogram = Data

Here is an example of a flowchart for deciding if the password entered by user matches the word "Python". For simplicity, the start and stop box shapes are not included in each flowchart in this book.

Ask the user to enter a password.

Is password equal to "Python"?

Yes

Print to screen that the password is correct.

No

Print to screen that the password is incorrect.

STOP

Use variables to store information from the user.

CREATE YOUR OWN CHATBOTS

Crunch numbers with powerful math functions.

STORING DATA WITH VARIABLES

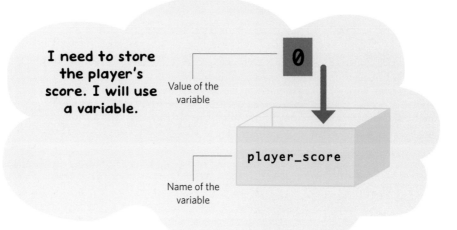

I need to store the player's score. I will use a variable.

Value of the variable

0

player_score

Name of the variable

Computers store information in memory so it can be used in programs. We call this information **data**. Sometimes, this data is provided by the user, and sometimes, it is generated as the program runs.

The data is stored in **variables**. Think of a variable as a box in the computer's memory. The name on the box is the name of the variable, and the contents of the box is the data that is stored, known as the **value** of the variable. You may have used variables in a math class, where they also represent data (an unknown number) but do not directly correspond to a storage location.

For example, a computer program may need to keep track of a player's score during a game. This can be stored in a variable called `player_score`. The image above shows an initial value of 0 (the score at the start of the game) being stored in the `player_score` variable.

Storing Variables in Python

In Python, a simple equal sign is used to store data in a variable.

To store the starting score of 0 in a variable with the name **player_score**, we use the following:

```
player_score = 0
```

Read this as "the **player_score** variable is set to 0," or "the **player_score** variable is assigned a value of 0." Do not read it as a mathematical equation or the next example will be very confusing!

As the game runs, the score changes, so the value in the variable must be changed. For example, the program may need to increase the player's score value by 1. The computer takes the old value stored in the variable **player_score**, adds 1 to it, and stores it back in **player_score**. The Python statement that does this is:

```
player_score = player_score + 1
```

To look at the what is stored in the variable at any time, you can just type in the variable name in the Python shell. It will return the value. So, type in **player_score** after each line.

```
>>> player_score = 0
>>> player_score
0
>>> player_score = player_score + 1
>>> player_score
1
```

If the information to be stored is text, single or double quotes are needed. Text is known as **strings** in Python.

```
name = 'Zoe'
```

WATCH YOUR SPELLING

If you try to access a variable that has not been assigned any value, you will get an error. So in the example on this page, you will get an error if you misspell the name of the variable. If you enter "Player_Score," for example, it will show an error because the variable name that was assigned is "player_score." Variable names are case sensitive.

NESTING QUOTES

If the text uses single or double quotes, you must use the other kind of quotation mark around it.

For example:

```
s = "Shelly's house"
action = 'She shouted "Go away!"'
```

YOU CAN ADD STRINGS

Python strings (text) can be added together to make longer strings.

For example:

```
>>> name = 'Zoe'
>>> message = 'likes to code'
>>> name + message
'Zoe likes to code'
```

Adding strings is often used to create new messages or information in a program. Sometimes a program may start with an empty string, shown as **''**, and add new information as it runs.

CHOOSE A GOOD NAME

The name of the variable should be something that makes it easy to remember what kind of data it stores. You could use **icecream** as a variable name for the player's score, but **player_score** is more descriptive and considered good programming practice. Similarly, you could use **x** as the name of the variable for the score, but a longer name such as **player_score** helps you remember how it is being used.

For longer names, Python programmers usually use lowercase text with an underscore, "_", to improve readability—for example, player_score. However, in some cases, programmers may use mixed case, like playerScore.

A variable name must follow some rules:

→ It cannot have spaces or special characters such as #, @, or the like.
→ It cannot start with a number.
→ It cannot be a word used as a Python function, for example *print*.

Let's take a look at some examples.

```
alien name = 'Speedy'
```

This will not work because the variable name has spaces. You will get a syntax error—Python telling you that it does not understand.

```
>>> alien name = 'Speedy'
SyntaxError: invalid syntax
```

However, you can use an underscore character or combine upper- and lowercases to make longer names.

```
alienName = 'Speedy'
```

This works; the variable name has no spaces.

```
alien_name = 'Speedy'
```

This also works; the variable name has no spaces.

GETTING DATA FROM THE USER

Computers get information from users in different ways. A user may provide information by typing into a keyboard, for example, or by clicking a mouse.

This data is usually stored in a variable so it can be used later.

This is the name of the variable that will get the information entered by the user. The information is always a string.

This is the prompt given to the user.

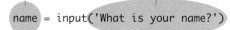

```
name = input('What is your name?')
```

Inputting Data in Python

To get information from the user via the keyboard, use the input function. This function takes the prompt given to the user and returns the information received from the user into a variable. For example:

Type the following into the Python shell:

```
name = input('What is your name?')
```

Then, type in your name and press Enter. If you type the variable **name** in the Python shell, you can see that the value stored in it is the information you entered. See below on how this works.

```
>>> name = input('What is your name?')
What is your name?Nico
>>> name
'Nico'
```

Note that the data entered by the user is always a string.

BIG IDEA
OUTPUTTING DATA ON A SCREEN

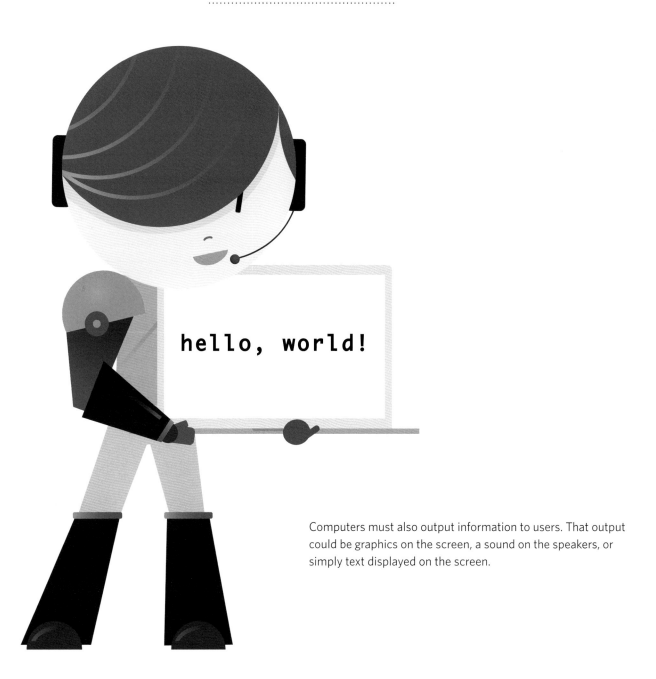

hello, world!

Computers must also output information to users. That output could be graphics on the screen, a sound on the speakers, or simply text displayed on the screen.

Outputting Data in Python

To output any information on the screen, use the **print** function. We saw this in the Introduction as the first line of Python code. The **print** function can be used to print out text, numbers, data stored in a variable, or a combination.

For strings:

```python
print('hello, world')
print("Shelly's friend")
```

For whole numbers (known as **integers** in Python):

```python
print(23)
```

For decimal numbers (known as **floats** in Python):

```python
print(3.14)
```

For data stored in a variable, use the name of the variable:

```python
print(player_score)
```

For multiple items, separate them with a comma:

```python
print('Your final score is', player_score)
print('Nice to meet you', username, '.')
```

This example of a print function uses multiple items, including variables that have been set earlier.

```python
>>> player_score = 100
>>> username = 'Zoe'
>>> print('Your final score is', player_score)
Your final score is 100
>>> print('Nice to meet you', username, '.')
Nice to meet you Zoe .
```

END CHARACTERS

By default, each print function creates a new line because the output by default ends with a new line character. You can change this by adding your own end characters. This is useful when you have multiple prints and you do not want them on separate lines. For example, to separate each print output with a comma, you can use:

```python
print(23, end=',')
```

ADDING COMMENTS TO YOUR CODE

What does this code do? I forget! I should have added comments.

Programmers add **comments** to make their code easier to read and change later.

Comments are notes written in a natural language, such as English, to help you remember how something was done or to explain it to other programmers who may use your code. Good programmers always add comments so they can easily fix or change their code later.

Adding Comments in Python

Comments are added by using a # symbol followed by the comment. The # and anything following it is ignored by the Python interpreter because it is not Python code, just a human readable note. Here are few examples.

```python
player_score = 0  # initialize score to 0 at start of game
# get name of user before game starts
player_name = input('Enter your name')
```

In this book, all comments will be shown using bold text. As you're trying out the example code on your computer, you do not have to enter the comments. You will find far more comments in the code in this book than what an average programmer may use because here they are used as a teaching tool to explain more about the code.

DOING MATH ON THE COMPUTER

Computers can crunch through numbers and do complex math. That's how they were first used, and it continues to be one of the most popular reasons to write programs. Today, we are interested in computing the large amount of data we generate each day as we use websites and apps. Having the ability to write a custom program to analyze data is useful in many applications.

Calculating in Python

The Python shell can be used as a powerful calculator. Type the following into the Python shell to experiment with basic math operations. Remember, you do not need to type in the comments—anything after and including #.

```
350 + 427  # addition
987 - 120  # subtraction
34 * 45  # multiplication is denoted by *
57 / 2  # division is denoted by /
57 // 2  # floor division- it discards the fractional part
57 % 2  # returns the remainder from the division
3 ** 2  # 3 raised to the power of 2
round(100/3, 2)  # round the result to 2 places
(100  - 5 * 3) / 5  # order of operations works as expected
```

```
350 + 427  # addition
987 - 120  # subtraction
```

Your results should look like the following:

```
>>> 350 + 427
777
>>> 987 - 120
867
>>> 34 * 45
1530
>>> 57 / 2
28.5
>>> 57 // 2
28
>>> 57 % 2
1
>>> 3 ** 2
9
>>> round(100/3, 2)
33.33
>>> (100 - 5 * 3) / 5
17.0
```

Using variables, we can store some numbers in memory and then use them in math. For example:

```
width = 100
height = 20
area = width * height   # area is width multiplied by height
print(area)
```

Please note that the above variables have numbers without a decimal point (known as integers).

You can also use numbers with decimal points, known as floats. Try the following in the Python shell:

```
distance = 102.52
speed = 20
time = distance / speed
time
```

Why 2 + 2 Is Sometimes 22!

When the user enters information, it is always text, even if it looks like a number!

Try entering the following into the Python shell.

```
number = input("Enter a number: ")
number + number
```

The variable **number** in the example (see below) appears to be an integer 2. However, it is actually text—a string "2". You can see it by entering **number** in the Python shell to see that it has quotation marks around it. In the example shown, the user entered 2, and it appears as '2.' So adding two strings results in concatenating the strings (combining two pieces of text); the '2' and '2' become '22'.

```
>>> number = input("Enter a number: ")
Enter a number: 2
>>> number + number
'22'
```

To treat the user entry as an integer, you must explicitly convert it from a string to an integer using the **int** function. For example, to convert the variable in this example to an integer and store it again in the same variable, **number**, do the following:

```
number = int(number)
```

To get the addition to work as expected, do the following:

```
number = input('Enter a number: ')
number = int(number)
number + number
```

See the output below of the Python shell experiment demonstrating the above.

```
>>> number = input("Enter a number: ")
Enter a number: 2
>>> number + number
'22'
>>> number
'2'
>>> number = int(number)
>>> number
2
>>> number + number
4
```

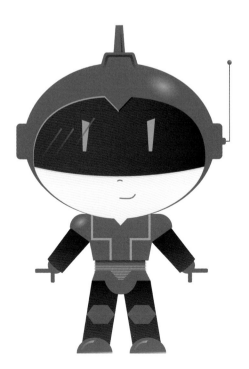

PROJECT
CREATE YOUR OWN CHATBOT

Let's now make a **chatbot**, a program that appears to talk intelligently to a human using text. Using the Big Ideas from this chapter, we will get user input and then respond to the user by putting information on the screen. Of course, because we are only in Chapter 1 of this book, this will be a simple chatbot. There will be ideas in subsequent chapters that you can use to make this chatbot better.

You can change the actual text of the chatbot responses or questions to customize it.

Note: There is no error checking for this program because it is the first program in this book. We assume the user will enter the correct input at each step. In subsequent chapters, you will learn some ways to check for errors.

THE ELIZA CHATBOT

A chatbot called ELIZA became famous in the 1960s. It illustrated something computer scientists were interested in—what it meant for a computer to be intelligent (learn more by reading about the Turing Test). ELIZA was successful by looking for patterns and giving related responses. It was able to fool many people, who thought it had human-like feelings.

Sample Run of the Chatbot

```
Hello. I am Zyxo 64. I am a chatbot
I like animals and I love to talk about food
What is your name?: Joe
Hello Joe , Nice to meet you
I am not very good at dates. What is the year?: 2019
Yes, I think that is correct. Thanks!
Can you guess my age? - enter a number: 15
Yes you are right. I am 15
I will be 100 in 85 years
That will be the year 2104
I love chocolate and I also like trying out new kinds of food
How about you? What is your favorite food?: pizza
I like pizza too.
How often do you eat pizza?: every day
Interesting.I wonder if that is good for your health
My favorite animal is a giraffe. What is yours?: turtle
turtle ! I do not like them.
I wonder if a turtle likes to eat pizza?:
How are you feeling today?: happy
Why are you feeling happy now?
Please tell me: start of a weekend
I understand. Thanks for sharing
It has been a long day
I am too tired to talk. We can chat again later.
Goodbye Joe I liked chatting with you
```

Step 1: Create a New File for Your Code

So far, we have used the Python shell to try out a few lines of code. Now that we are making a project that we want to save and edit easily, we will use a file to enter the code.

❶ Click on File > New File.

❷ In the new window, enter a comment—a human readable note to yourself on what this project is about.

❸ Click on File > Save As and save it on your computer with the name **Chatbot.py** (or any other name; this is just a suggestion).

❹ You can run the code by clicking on Run > Run Module.

The file ending in .py indicates that it is a Python file. You can run this Python file by clicking on Run > Run Module and also from a command line interface on any computer that has Python installed. For example, you can run the project from a terminal window on Unix or Mac using **python3 Chatbot.py**.

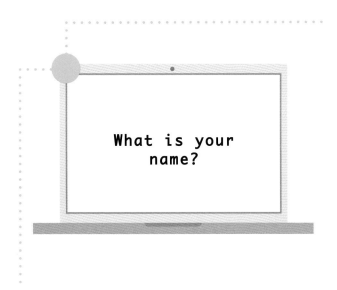

Step 3:
Showcase Your Math Coding Skills

To show that your chatbot can do math (and you can try out the Python math functions), ask the user for the current year and a guess of the chatbot's age. Then, respond with the year in which the chatbot will be 100. (You can easily change this to asking the user for their age and telling them the year they will be 100.)

Pseudocode

Get current year from user
Get chatbot age from user
Print guess is correct
Convert chatbot age to integer
Set years to 100 - chatbot age
Print I will be 100 in years
Convert current year to integer
Print That will be current year + years

Python Code at End of Step 3

```
# get year information
year = input('I am not very good at dates. What \
is the year?: ')
print('Yes, I think that is correct. Thanks! ')

# ask user to guess age
myage = input('Can you guess my age? - enter a \
number: ')
print('Yes you are right. I am ', myage)

# do math to calculate when chatbot will be 100
myage = int(myage)
nyears = 100 - myage
print('I will be 100 in', nyears, 'years')
print('That will be the year', int(year) + \
nyears)
```

Add the code above to your file and then test it by clicking on Run > Run Module.

Step 2:
Add Code for the Introductions

To start, the chatbot introduces itself using print statements and asks the user for their name using an input statement. The name entered by the user is stored in a variable called **name** and used again later to print a custom message.

Pseudocode

Print introduction to the chatbot
Get name from user
Print hello name

Python Code at End of Step 1

```
# chatbot introduction
print('Hello. I am Zyxo 64. I am a chatbot')
print('I like animals and I love to talk about food')
name = input('What is your name?: ')
print('Hello', name, ', Nice to meet you')
```

Add the code above to your file and then test it by clicking on Run > Run Module.

Step 4:
Use Data Stored for Simple Fill-in Template Responses

We can now ask and respond to the user on a few topics, using the data entered by the user where possible in the conversation. Here is an example of a conversation on food and another one on animals. Notice how the responses entered by the user are stored in variables and reused in the print statements.

```
# food conversation
print('I love chocolate and I also like trying out new kinds of food')
food = input('How about you? What is your favorite food?: ')
print('I like', food, 'too.')
question = 'How often do you eat ' + food + '?: '
howoften = input(question)
print('Interesting. I wonder if that is good for your health')

# animal conversation
animal = input('My favorite animal is a giraffe. What is yours?: ')
print(animal,'! I do not like them.')
print('I wonder if a', animal, 'likes to eat', food, '?')
```

Add the code above to your file and then test it by clicking on Run > Run Module.

I will be 100
in 2104

I like chocolate.
What about you?

Yummy!

How you are feeling?

Step 5:
Add in a Conversation About Feelings

Add in some more general comments on how the user is feeling, responding with a generic comment so the chatbot does not have to make an actual intelligent response based on the user's input.

```
# conversation about feelings
feeling = input('How are you feeling today?: ')
print('Why are you feeling', feeling, 'now?')
reason = input('Please tell me: ')
print('I understand. Thanks for sharing')
```

Add the code above to your file and then test it by clicking on Run > Run Module.

Step 6:
Close with a Custom Goodbye

Close the chatbot conversation with a custom goodbye using the user's name.

```
# goodbye
print('It has been a long day')
print('I am too tired to talk. We can chat again later.')
print('Goodbye', name, 'I liked chatting with you')
```

Add the code above to your file and then test it by clicking on Run > Run Module.

GOODBYE

How Can You Make This Chatbot Better?

One of the biggest problems with this project's code is that the computer does not have any choice on what output to give. It cannot decide to do a different output based on the input. In order to do this, the chatbot must make decisions. We will learn to do this with conditional statements in Chapter 3.

To make this chatbot more interesting, we may want to add some unpredictability so it says something different each time it runs. We will be able to do that after we look at lists and the random module in Chapter 4.

The chatbot can be improved by adding in a few pauses so that it seems like it is thinking. You will learn how to do this in Chapter 3.

At the end of Chapter 3 and again at end of Chapter 4, come back to this project and add code to make your chatbot a bit more intelligent and useful.

This chatbot is yours; you can customize it and make it more humanlike by using your creativity and a bit of Python code.

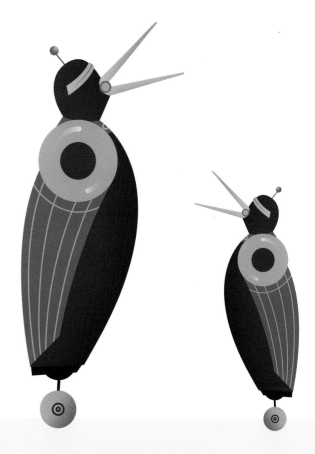

USEFUL CHATBOTS

There are several chatbots in use today that can handle simple conversations and are used in sales, customer support, and other applications. With more advances in computing, chatbots understand not just typed text but also human speech. They can rely on large amounts of data to reply intelligently and can respond not just in text but in a human's voice.

EXPERIMENT AND EXTEND

MAD LIBS

Mad Libs is a classic game invented in the 1950s by Stern and Price. One player asks others for a list of words, uses them to fill in blanks in a story, and then reads out the usually funny or silly story or sentence. Stern and Price's original Mad Libs book has the following example:

"(exclamation)! he said (adverb) as he jumped into his convertible (noun) and drove off with his (adjective) wife."

Experiment 1:
Mad Libs

Using the idea of storing user input into variables and using them in new output, you can create a version of the classic Mad Libs game.

Pseudocode

Get nouns, verbs, etc., from the user
Print Mad Lib sentences using responses

Sample Run

```
Name an object in this room: table
What kind of food do you like?: pizza
What is your favorite color: green
Enter a name of a zoo animal: giraffe


The giraffe jumped onto the green table and flew
across the city to eat pizza at his favorite
restaurant.
```

Experiment 2:
Song Lyrics Generator

Create a song by using a template and filling in a series of words that are entered by the user. Get meaningful entries from the user by giving hints to make sure the words work well in the song.

Pseudocode

Get words for song from user
Print song with responses filled into template

Sample Run

```
Enter something plural that is red. example roses: cherries
Enter something plural that is blue. example violets: oceans
Enter something plural you love. example puppies: baby pandas
Enter a verb such as jumping, singing: dancing
-------------------
cherries are red
oceans are blue
I like baby pandas
But not as much as I love dancing with you!
```

Experiment 3:
Unit Converter

Create a program that takes information in inches, pounds, and Fahrenheit (system of measurements used in the United States) and then converts it to cm, kg, and Celsius (the metric system of measurement).

Pseudocode

Get inches from user
Convert inches to integer
Set cm to inches x 2.54
Print cm
Get pounds from user
Convert pounds to integer
Set kg to pounds / 2.2
Print kg
Get fahrenheit from user
Convert fahrenheit to integer
Set celsius to fahrenheit - 32 / (9/5)
Print celsius

Sample Run

```
Enter distance in inches: 102
102 inches is equal to 259.08 cm
Enter weight in pounds: 145
145 pounds is equal to 65.91 kg
Enter temperature in Fahrenheit: 70
70 Fahrenheit is equal to 21.11 Celsius
```

Experiment 4:
Restaurant Bill Calculator

Ask the user for the total of the restaurant bill, what percentage tip they want to give, and the number of people the bill is to be shared between. Give the total tip and total amount, followed by the tip amount per person and total of the bill per person.

Pseudocode

Get bill amount from user
Get tip percentage from user
Get number of people from user
Convert all user input to integers
Set tip amount to tip bill amount x (percentage / 100)
Set total amount to bill amount + tip amount
Print tip per person , tip amount / number of people
Print total per person, total amount / number of people

Sample Run

```
What is the total on the bill?: 55
What % tip would you like to give?: 15
How many people are sharing the bill?: 4
Tip amount =  8.25
Total bill =  63.25
-------------------------
Tip amount per person =  2.06
Total amount per person =  15.81
```

Experiment 5:
Paint Calculator

Ask the user for the length, width, and height of a room in feet and ask for the number of doors and windows. Give them the total area to be painted and the amount of paint needed for the walls, assuming you can subtract 20 square feet for each door and 15 square feet for each window and that the paint coverage is 350 square feet per gallon.

Pseudocode

Get height, width, length from user
Get number of windows, doors from user
Set wall area to (2 x length x height) + (2 x width x height)
Set NoPaintArea to 20 x doors + 15 x windows
Set PaintArea to wall area - NoPaintArea
Print PaintArea
Set gallons to wall area / 350
Print gallons after rounding to 2 places

Sample Run

```
Enter length of the room in feet: 24
Enter width of the room in feet: 14
Enter height of the room in feet: 9
Enter number of doors: 2
Enter number of windows: 4
Total surface area to paint 584
Number of gallons of paint needed 1.67
```

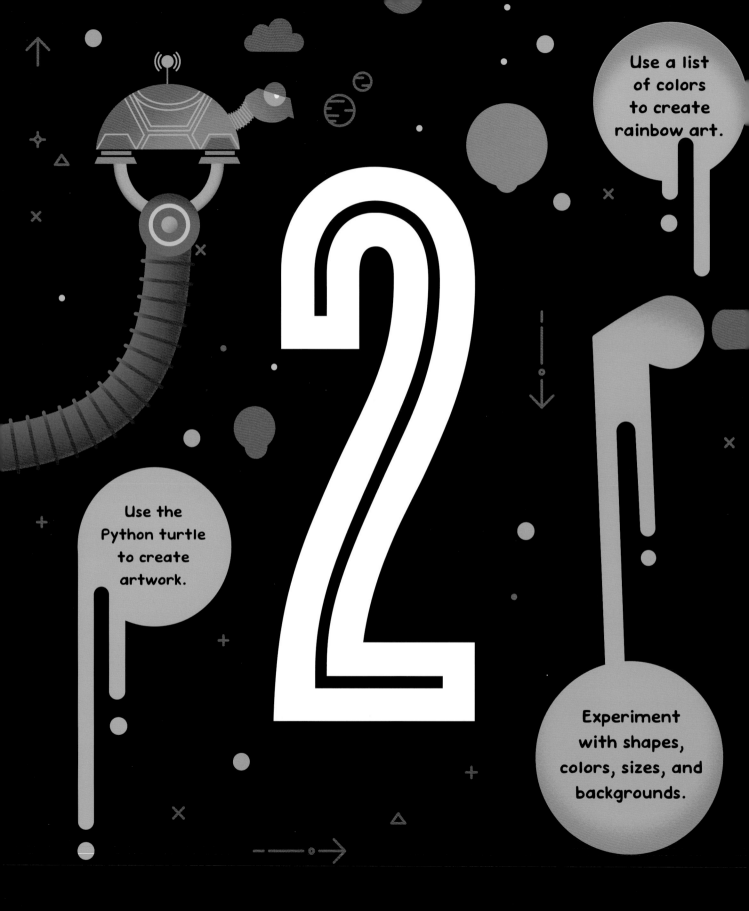

Use loops to repeat shapes and create intricate geometric patterns that are only possible in code.

CREATE YOUR OWN ART MASTERPIECES

Use your creativity to make drawings of faces, houses, and more.

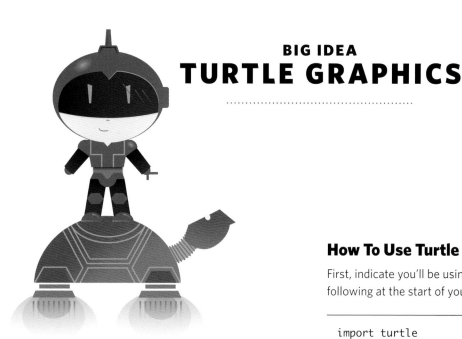

Using turtle graphics is a fun way to learn Python and create artwork using code.

The virtual turtle is a screen cursor depicted by a triangle that can draw on the screen by entering instructions. These instructions are known as functions (see Introduction for more on Python functions) and they include:

➔ Moving in all directions
➔ Turning in all directions
➔ Changing colors
➔ Lifting and putting down the pen
➔ Moving to any part of the screen

These functions can be combined to create complex art pieces. For example, a function to move the turtle forward 100 steps creates a line in its path. All movements are relative to the turtle's current position.

WHY A TURTLE?

Turtle graphics was inspired by a robot called a turtle that was controlled by the LOGO programming language. LOGO was developed by Seymour Papert, Wally Feurzeig, and Cynthia Solomon in 1967. Their work continues to inspire many programming languages used in education today.

How To Use Turtle Graphics in Python

First, indicate you'll be using turtle graphics by entering the following at the start of your code:

```
import turtle
```

This **imports**, or brings into your program and makes available, a module in Python that has all the functions for the turtle. Modules of this kind are extensions to Python that have functions for a specific application; in this case, it's a module with functions to use turtle graphics.

In order to do anything with the turtle, you must first create one and assign it to a variable. Think of the variable as a name for the turtle. In the examples in this book, we call our turtle "shelly," but you can use any word or name as the variable.

```
shelly = turtle.Turtle()
```

Type the above two lines of Python into the Python shell. You should see a new window open. This is the turtle graphics window, with a small triangle turtle in the center.

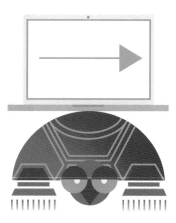

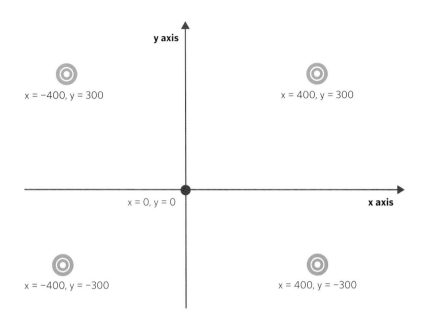

x = −400, y = 300

y axis

x = 400, y = 300

x = 0, y = 0

x axis

x = −400, y = −300

x = 400, y = −300

You can now control the turtle by giving it instructions (functions). Enter the following Python functions into the Python shell one line at a time to see what they do. To make it easier, move the windows so you can see the Python shell window and the turtle graphics window next to each other and watch the drawing change as you enter each line of code.

```
shelly.forward(100)  # moves shelly forward 100 steps
shelly.right(90)  # turns shelly right 90 degrees
shelly.left(60)  # turns shelly left 60 degrees
shelly.backward(100)  # moves shelly backward 100 steps
shelly.color('red')  # makes shelly draw in color red
shelly.circle(10)  # makes shelly draw a circle of size 10
shelly.penup()  # makes shelly lift pen
shelly.pendown()  # makes shelly put the pen down to draw
shelly.reset()  # clears screen and goes back to start position
shelly.goto(35, 80)  # move to x coordinate 35,y coordinate 80
shelly.hideturtle()  # makes shelly not visible on the screen
```

The center of the window is the *x* coordinate 0 and the *y* coordinate 0. See the diagram above for other sample points in the turtle graphics window.

CHANGING THE TURTLE'S SHAPE

You can change the turtle's shape from the classic triangle to a more realistic-looking turtle by entering:

```
shelly.shape('turtle')
```

HOW TO FIND YOUR LOCATION IN TURTLE GRAPHICS

You can always find out where you are by printing out the current coordinates.

```
print(shelly.xcor(), shelly.ycor())
```

Computer screens can vary, so some of the examples in the book may appear a little different on your computer. You can check the size of the screen by entering the following in the Python shell:

```
turtle.screensize()
```

BIG IDEA
LOOPS

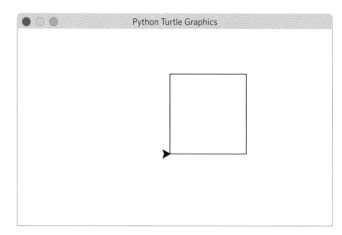

Python Turtle Graphics

Let's take an example of the turtle drawing a square on the screen like the one shown above.

Starting at the turtle's current location, functions must be entered to move it and turn it at right angles (90 degrees). Imagine yourself holding a pen and walking on a large sheet of paper to make marks.

Here are the commands in pseudocode to make a square of size 100:

Pseudocode

> **move 100 steps forward**
> **turn 90 degrees to the left**
> **move 100 steps forward**
> **turn 90 degrees to the left**
> **move 100 steps forward**
> **turn 90 degrees to the left**
> **move 100 steps forward**
> **turn 90 degrees to the left**

The code above is repetitive. Do you see the pattern? There are two lines that are repeated 4 times, one for each side of the square.

Computers are good at repeating anything. All programming languages have a built-in ability to repeat a set of instructions called a **loop**.

This can be written in pseudocode more simply as:

Pseudocode

> **repeat 4 times the following:**
> **move 100 steps forward**
> **turn 90 degrees to the left**

Note that in the pseudocode, the two instructions that must be repeated are indented.

How to Use Loops in Python

To repeat something a fixed number of times, we use a **for loop**. The code after the statement with a **for** in it is indented to show that it is the block that repeats (IDLE will automatically indent this). The Python code for the above pseudocode is:

```python
for i in range (4):
  shelly.forward(100)
  shelly.left(90)
```

Add a print function to the above code so that it prints the variable **i** and runs it again. Here's what your code will look like:

```python
for i in range(4):
  shelly.forward(100)
  shelly.left(90)
  print(i)  # Add this NEW LINE
```

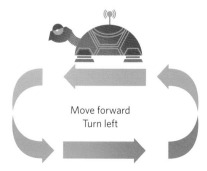

Move forward
Turn left

Repeat this loop 4 times

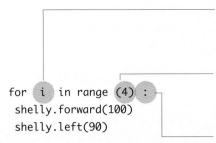

```
for  i  in range (4) :
    shelly.forward(100)
    shelly.left(90)
```

This is a variable that's a counter in the loop. It's called **i** in this example, but you can use any variable name.

This is the number of times this loop will repeat. The counter starts at 0 and will go up by 1 till it reaches this number.

Notice the **:** at the end of this line. Once entered, the next line of code must be indented to show that it's the code that repeats.

You should see the turtle draw a square in the turtle graphics window again and print the numbers 0, 1, 2, and 3 in the Python shell, as shown below.

```
0
1
2
3
```

Remember, the variable is called **i** in these examples, but you can use any variable name.

Adding Color

To color in the square, you must call the function **begin_fill** and set a color before the shape is drawn and then end with an **end_fill** function.

Below is the complete code required to create a red square. You can enter this in the Python shell line by line or create a new file in the editor and run it.

```
# red square
import turtle
shelly = turtle.Turtle()
shelly.begin_fill()  # start filling shape
shelly.color('red')  # use color red
for i in range(4):
  shelly.forward(100)
  shelly.left(90)
shelly.end_fill()  # end filling shape
```

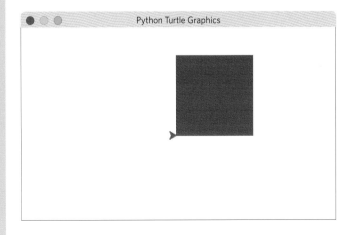

MORE ABOUT FOR LOOPS

The **for** loop in the examples in this chapter are simple and are used to repeat something a fixed number of times. So to repeat something 4 times, we use **for i in range(4)**. The 4 in **range(4)** is the stop value; by default, the start value is 0, so **i** takes the values 0, 1, 2, and 3.

→ It's possible to change the start value. For example, **for i in range(1,5)** will start counting at 1 and stop at 5. So **i** takes the values 1, 2, 3, and 4.

→ You can also change the steps of the increment. For example, **for i in range(1,10,2)** will start counting at 1, stop before 10, and go up in steps of 2. So **i** takes the values 1, 3, 5, 7, and 9.

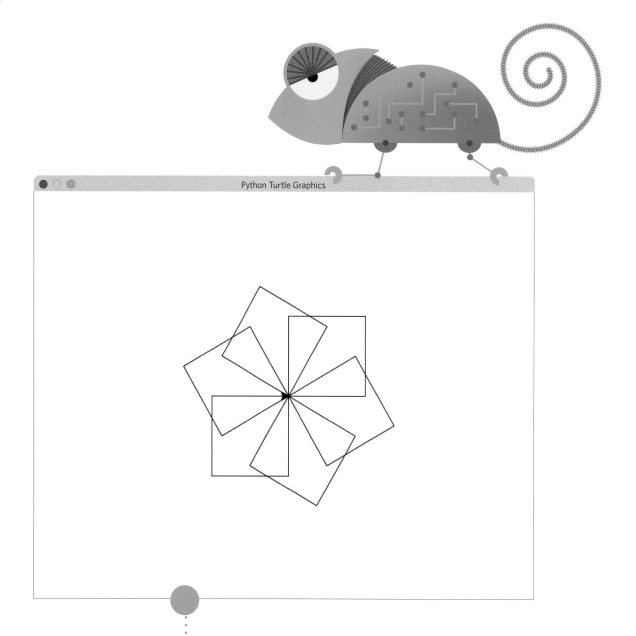

Python Turtle Graphics

Nested Loops

Look at this shape. Can you see it is a series of squares, each turned a little (exactly 60 degrees, actually)? To make this, we can use the loop above to make the square and then repeat that loop six times, with a 60 degree turn in between each repetition. We will repeat something that itself repeats.

HOW TO FORCE YOUR CODE TO STOP RUNNING

If your code is running and you must stop it at any time, you can move your mouse to the Python shell and enter a Control+C to break out and force an abrupt stop of the program. This is helpful when you realize you have made a mistake in the turtle graphics program and you do not want it to finish, or as we will learn in Chapter 3, you create an infinite loop and the program is never going to stop.

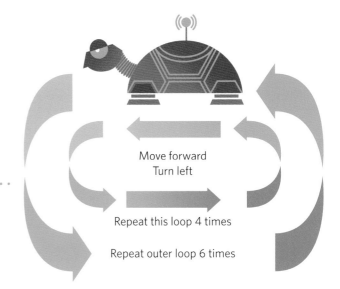

Move forward
Turn left

Repeat this loop 4 times

Repeat outer loop 6 times

This is called a **nested loop**, a loop within a loop.

Here is the pseudocode to draw this shape. As you can see, the loop for the square is inside the loop that repeats 6 times.

Pseudocode

repeat 6 times the following:
    repeat 4 times the following:
        move 100 steps forward
        turn 90 degrees to the left
    turn 60 degrees to the right

Nested Loops in Python

The code for the above is:

```python
# outer loop repeats the square 6 times
for n in range(6):
    # inner loop repeats 4 times to make a square
    for i in range(4):
        shelly.forward(100)
        shelly.left(90)
    shelly.right(60)  # add a turn before the next square
```

Experiment by changing the numbers in the code above. Instead of the outer loop repeating 6 times, what happens if you change it to 100 times? What else will you need to change to make the squares closer together?

BIG IDEA
STORING DATA
IN LISTS

A computer can store a collection of items in a list. In this chapter, we will store the names of colors that we need for a rainbow drawing into a list called colors. A list is a special variable that has multiple items, which we can access one at a time. Think of a list as a storage location that looks like a series of boxes or shelves in a bookshelf.

Computers number items in a list starting at 0. The first item is the 0th item in the list.

To get to each color, the computer can use an index or counter to step through the list, pulling out one item at a time.

To store the color red in the first item in the list called colors, the computer assigns red to the 0th position in this list.

To get the color red, the computer can then access item 0 in the list.

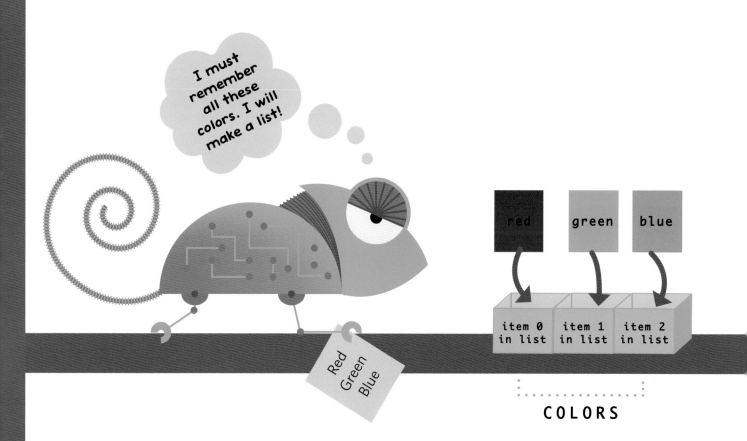

COLORS

How to Set Up a List in Python

The code to set up the list is as follows:

```
colors = ['red', 'green', 'blue']
```

Notice how the list is enclosed with square brackets and how each item, in this case name of color, is separated by a comma. Because each color name is a piece of text, it is written in quotation marks.

Lists in Python are indexed starting at 0. So to access the color red, we need to get the 0th item in the list, which is accessed by using **colors[0]**. Type the following, one line at a time, into the Python shell to test it out:

```
colors = ['red', 'green', 'blue']
colors[0]
colors[1]
```

This is what you should get:

```
>>> colors = ['red', 'green', 'blue']
>>> colors[0]
'red'
>>> colors[1]
'green'
```

You can change the color for your turtle by taking a color from the list. For example, to get red you would use:

```
shelly.color(colors[0])
```

To get each color in order, you need to get the 0th color, 1st color, 2nd color, and so on—basically the color corresponding to the counter in the loop. If the counter in our loop is **i**, we would use the following to get the **i**th color.

```
shelly.color(colors[i])
```

Try this by entering the following code. You should see three lines, one for each color printed in the Python shell.

```
colors = ['red', 'green', 'blue']
for i in range(3):
    shelly.color(colors[i])
    shelly.forward(50)
    print(colors[i])
```

We will use this idea in our project to draw rainbow patterns.

Note: Python lists are very powerful, and we can use them in many ways. We will learn more about using lists in Chapter 4.

PROJECT
CREATING GEOMETRIC ART

Step 1: Make a Hexagon

To begin any turtle project, import the turtle module so you can use the functions. You must also create a turtle (see page 38).

Start a new file called Art.py, enter the following code, and run it to make sure you get a turtle. Add a comment line on the top to remind you of the project. Adding comments is good programming practice.

```
# make a geometric pattern
import turtle
shelly = turtle.Turtle()
```

Now, let's modify the pseudocode on how to make a square (see page 40) so we can make a hexagon. The number of sides is 6, and the angle to turn is now 60 degrees.

Pseudocode

repeat 6 times the following:
move 100 steps forward
turn 60 degrees to the left

To complete Step 1, your Python code should look like this:

```
# make a geometric pattern
import turtle
shelly = turtle.Turtle()
# repeat 6 times - move forward and turn
for i in range(6) :
  shelly.forward(100)
  shelly.left(60)
```

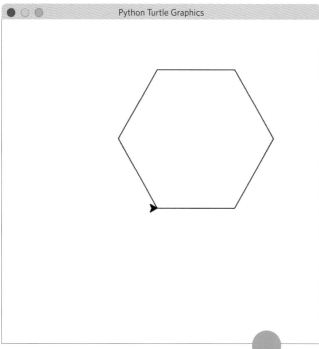

Python Turtle Graphics

Step 1: hexagon with triangular turtle

Step 2: Repeat the Hexagon Using a Nested Loop

Now that we have a hexagon using a loop, we can put this hexagon code inside another loop that repeats, to get a number of hexagons arranged in a circle, each slightly overlapping each other.

Modifying the pseudocode from Step 1, we can turn each hexagon just 10 degrees from the previous one. To complete the circle, we need to do this a total of 360 ÷ 10 = 36 times (360 is the total number of degrees in a circle).

Pseudocode

repeat 36 times the following:
    repeat 6 times the following:
        move 100 steps forward
        turn 60 degrees to the left
    Turn at 10 degrees to the right

Step 2: nested loop hexagon

You can select the **for** loop code from your previous project and press Tab to indent it (or select and click on Format > Indent Region on IDLE).

Then, add the **for n in range(36):** on top and the **shelly.right(10)** below it to handle the other part of the pseudocode.

Remember, the comments after the # are optional. They only explain to the programmer what the code is doing.

To complete Step 2, your Python code should look like this:

```python
# make a geometric pattern
import turtle
shelly = turtle.Turtle()
for n in range(36):
# repeat 6 times - move forward and turn
  for i in range(6) :
    shelly.forward(100)
    shelly.left(60)
  shelly.right(10)   # add a turn
```

Step 3:
Change the Background;
Add Rainbow Colors

You can make this drawing more interesting by adding colors and a background. Here's the code you need to change the background color:

```
turtle.bgcolor('black')   # turn background black
```

In the Big Idea section on page 44, we saw that the computer can store related items in a list—like a list of colors. We also saw how **colors[0]** gives the first item in the list, **colors[1]** give the second item, and so on. We can use the loop to go from item 0 to item 1 and print all the colors in the list. The "**i**" in the for loop is a counter, which starts at 0 and stops before 6. Using **colors[i]** gives us the **i**th item in the list.

Step 3: nested loop hexagon with background and rainbow colors

The new line of code to add inside the loop for the hexagon is:

```
shelly.color(colors[i])
```

To use different colors in the drawing, you'll need to modify the code so the turtle color is changed inside the loop. Here's the final code to make this rainbow pattern:

```python
# make a geometric rainbow pattern
import turtle
# pick order of colors for the hexagon
colors = ['red', 'yellow', 'blue', 'orange', \
'green', 'red']
shelly = turtle.Turtle()
turtle.bgcolor('black')   # turn background black
# make 36 hexagons, each 10 degrees apart
for n in range(36):
# make hexagon by repeating 6 times
  for i in range(6):
    shelly.color(colors[i])   # pick color at position i
    shelly.forward(100)
    shelly.left(60)
# add a turn before the next hexagon
  shelly.right(10)
```

Step 4:
Add Small White Circles Around the Pattern

You can also make the turtle go to the outer edge of the pattern, make a small circle, return to the center, and then repeat, going all the way around the pattern. This is fun to watch, and it adds an extra detail to the art that's very easy to do in code but not so easy to create using any other art medium.

This step demonstrates the turtle moving forward and returning by going backward to its start position. Since there are 36 hexagons, we'll draw 36 small circles to match; each time the turtle returns to the center, it turns 10 degrees: 36 x 10 = 360 degrees, to make a complete circle around the pattern.

Add the following code to the end of the code in Step 3:

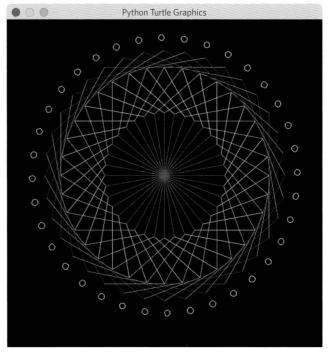

Step 4: nested loop hexagon with background, rainbow colors, and small white circles

```
# get ready to draw 36 circles
shelly.penup()
shelly.color('white')
# repeat 36 times to match the 36 hexagons
for i in range(36):
  shelly.forward(220)
  shelly.pendown()
  shelly.circle(5)
  shelly.penup()
  shelly.backward(220)
  shelly.right(10)
# hide turtle to finish the drawing
shelly.hideturtle()
```

EXPERIMENT AND EXTEND

Experiment 1:
Create a Row of Colored Squares

Start with this pseudocode to try creating a row of colored squares:

Pseudocode

repeat 6 times the following:
    Set color from list
    Repeat 4 times the following:
        Move forward 20
        Turn left 90
    Put pen up
    Move forward 30
    Put pen down
Hide turtle

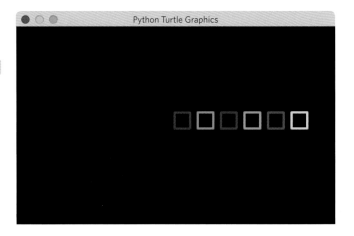

Experiment 3:
Make a Green Face with Circles

Can you make this green face using a series of circles? To help get you started, here's the code for making one eye:

```
shelly.goto(-30,100)
shelly.begin_fill()
shelly.color('white')
shelly.circle(30)
shelly.end_fill()
shelly.begin_fill()
shelly.color('black')
shelly.circle(20)
shelly.end_fill()
```

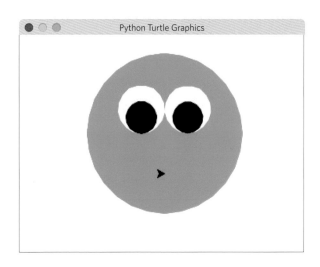

Experiment 2:
Make a House with Starter Code

Start with the following code, which creates one filled gray square and one filled red triangle:

```
# make a house
import turtle
turtle.bgcolor('blue')
shelly = turtle.Turtle()
# make the first big square for house
shelly.begin_fill()  # start fill of color
shelly.color('gray')
for i in range(4):
  shelly.forward(100)
  shelly.left(90)
shelly.end_fill()  # end fill of color
shelly.penup()
shelly.goto(-20,100)  # move turtle to next area
shelly.pendown()
# make a red triangle roof
shelly.begin_fill()  # start fill for roof
shelly.color('red')
shelly.left(60)
shelly.forward(140)
shelly.right(120)
shelly.forward(140)
shelly.right(120)
shelly.forward(140)
shelly.end_fill()  # end fill of color for roof
# make a window
shelly.penup()
shelly.goto(25,80)  # move to window position
shelly.pendown()
shelly.begin_fill()  # start filling window color
shelly.color('yellow')
for i in range(4):
  shelly.forward(20)
  shelly.left(90)
shelly.end_fill()  # end filling window color
# hide the turtle when done
shelly.hideturtle()
```

Experiment 4:
Overlapping Circles

Change the code at the end of Step 2 in this chapter's project to create a different image. Use the following:

Pseudocode

repeat 36 times the following:

> **Make a circle of size 100**
>
> **Turn 10 degrees to the right**

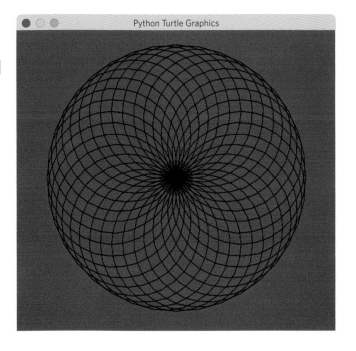

Experiment 5:
Circle of Circles

Change the code at end of Step 4 to make multiple circles coming back. Use the following:

Pseudocode

repeat 36 times the following

> **Lift pen**
>
> **Move forward 200**
>
> **Repeat 6 times**
>
> > **Put pen down**
> >
> > **Make a circle of size 5**
> >
> > **Put pen up**
> >
> > **Move back 20**
>
> **Move back to center 80**
>
> **Turn 10 degrees to the right**

Hide turtle

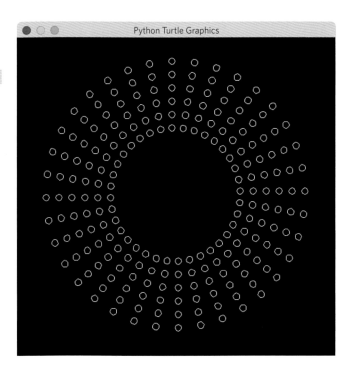

More to Explore

Can you make one or more of these images? Some are related to the other challenges in this chapter.

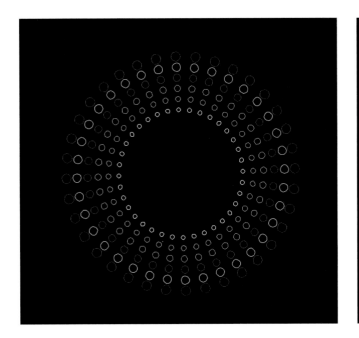

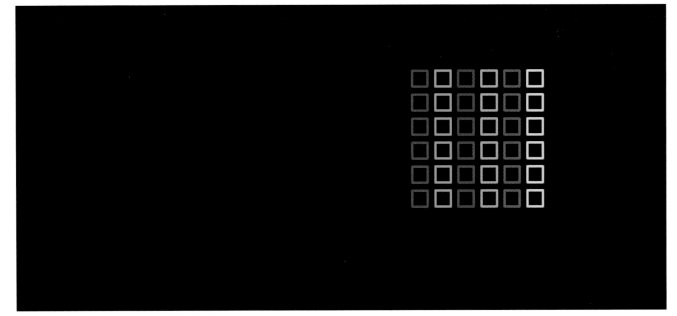

Run code based on user's choice.

Repeat tasks until you are ready to quit.

3

Use your creativity and write your own interactive fiction.

Make a custom quiz game for friends and family.

CREATE YOUR OWN ADVENTURE GAMES

COMPUTERS UNDERSTAND TRUE AND FALSE

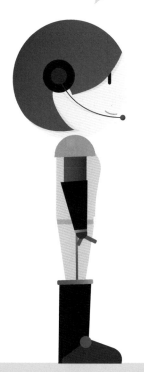

24 is an even number.

Python is simple to learn.

312 is less than 123.

True.

True.

False.

BOOLEAN VALUES

True and false are known as Boolean values or Booleans, after English mathematician George Boole. His invention of Boolean algebra in the mid 1800s is the basis of modern digital computer logic.

Computers can decide if a statement is true or false. For example, the statement "24 is an even number" is true, but the statement "25 is an even number" is false.

Computers use this true and false value to determine which part of the algorithm (which code) must be executed.

In the Introduction, we saw how decisions can be shown using a diamond shaped box. In this example, based on whether the statement "R is equal to 0" is true or false, the algorithm chooses two different paths and gives two different answers.

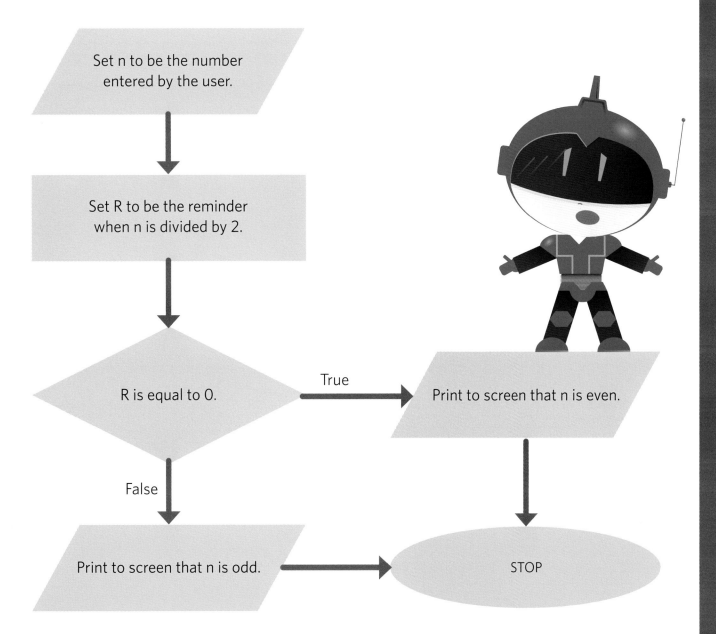

Set n to be the number entered by the user.

Set R to be the reminder when n is divided by 2.

R is equal to 0.

True

Print to screen that n is even.

False

Print to screen that n is odd.

STOP

Comparing Items in Python

We use two equal signs (see below) to compare two items. The result is the value **True** if they are indeed the same or the value **False** if they are not.

Try this in the Python shell:

```
>>> player_score = 0  # this puts 0 into the variable player_score
>>> player_score == 0  # this checks if value in player_score is 0
```

Because player_score is set to 0, when it is compared with 0, Python shell returns **True**.

If the information to be tested is text (a string), the check is case sensitive. In the example below, variable name stores "Zoe" with an uppercase "Z" and it is tested against "zoe" with a lowercase "z". They are not the same, the check fails, and Python returns **False**.

```
>>> name = 'Zoe'  # set the variable name to the value Zoe
>>> name == 'zoe'
False
>>>
```

We can also use other comparison operators to check if something is true or false. Here are some examples.

```
>>> 5 > 2  # check if 5 is greater than 2
True
```

```
>>> 5 < 2  # check if 5 is less than 2
False
```

```
>>> 5 != 3  # check if 5 is not equal to 3
True
```

```
>>> choice = 'yes'
>>> choice != 'quit'  # check if choice is not equal to quit
True
```

BOOLEAN EXPRESSIONS

Any statement that evaluates to True or False is called a **Boolean expression** or a **condition**. Examples include:

```
x < 2
choice == 'yes'
player_score > 100
```

COMPUTERS CAN COMBINE TRUE AND FALSE

Take an umbrella.

Often, we combine different conditions to create a new condition to help us make our decision. For example, we need to check on the condition "It is raining" AND the condition "I have an umbrella" before we decide to take an umbrella with us when we go out. We are using the word AND to combine the two conditions—raining and having an umbrella.

Computers combine Boolean expressions that can be true or false, using the Boolean operators—AND, OR, NOT—to create new true and false Boolean expressions.

AND OPERATOR

If we know that "It is raining" is true AND we know that "I have an umbrella" is also true, we know we can take our umbrella with us when we step outside.

So, "take umbrella" is true only if *both* statements are true.

OR OPERATOR

If we know that "It is windy" is true OR if we know that "It is cold" is true, we can decide that we should take a jacket. We will also take our jacket if it is cold, if it is windy, or if it is both cold and windy.

So, "take jacket" is true if *any one* of the statements or both statements are true.

NOT OPERATOR

If we know that "It is warm outside" is false (it is NOT true), we can decide that we should take a jacket.

So "take jacket" is true if "it is warm outside" is false; it is the *opposite*.

Using Operators in Python

We can use the **AND** operator (and) to combine two Booleans.

For example: The game can proceed if both the number of lives (stored in variable `lives`) and amount of time left in game (stored in variable **game_time**) are greater than 0.

```
>>> lives > 0 and game_time > 0
# game proceeds only if there are lives and time left
```

We can also use the **OR** operator (or) to combine two Booleans.

For example: The game must end if either number of lives (stored in variable **lives**) is equal to 0 or if there is no time left; that is, the amount of time left in the game (stored in variable **game_time**) is equal to 0.

```
>>> lives == 0 or game_time == 0
# game stops if no lives left or there is no time left
```

We use the **NOT** operator (!) to get the opposite value.

```
>>> choice != 'quit'  # user does not want to quit
>>> not(player_score == 0)  # this true if player_score is not a 0
```

TRUE WITH A CAPITAL T

True and False are recognized in Python as Boolean values, and they are case sensitive. Try the following in the Python shell:

```
>>> True and True
>>> true or true
```

The second expression gives an error because "true" is not a Boolean; it is considered a variable that has not been assigned any value yet.

BIG IDEA
CODE BASED ON CONDITIONS

We make decisions and execute different actions based on something being true or false.

For example, consider a decision you may make at breakfast time: If there are eggs in the refrigerator and I have time (both have to be true), I will make a fried egg for breakfast and then sit down and eat it. Else, I will take a granola bar to eat on the way. Based on the condition being true or false, you do different actions.

Similarly, computers execute code based on a **condition**, a Boolean expression that evaluates to true or false. If the condition evaluates to true, one set of code statements (the *if* block of code) is executed; else, the other part (the *else* block of code) is executed. This kind of statement is called a **conditional** or an **if-else statement**.

Using a flowchart, the breakfast example can be shown as follows:

True . . . If block of code

False . . . Else block of code

I have eggs in the refrigerator AND I have time.

True → Make fried eggs. Make toast. Eat eggs and toast for breakfast.

False → Pick up granola bar from kitchen shelf. Put granola bar in bag to eat later.

Make an egg?

Make instant oatmeal?

Take a granola bar to go?

Using Conditional Statements in Python

To execute code based on a condition, we use an **if statement**, also known as a **conditional statement**. If the condition is true, it executes the set of statements in the if section; otherwise, it executes the statements in the else section. *The else part is optional.*

Conditional (If-Else) Statements

Try this in the Python shell:

```
>>> raining = True
>>> if raining:
        print('It is wet outside')
        print('Wear rain boots')
        print('Take an umbrella')
```

```
It is wet outside
Wear rain boots
Take an umbrella
>>>
```

Run the above code again, and this time set raining to be False. Nothing will print.

Here is an example that asks the user for the day of the week and depending on the day, sets an alarm variable and prints a message. In the example below, the user entered the day as Monday, so it printed the message, "Get up and get ready for work."

```
>>> day = input('enter day of the week ')
enter day of the week monday
>>> if day == 'saturday' or day == 'sunday':
        alarm = 'OFF'
        print('It is a weekend - sleep in!')
else:
        alarm = 'ON'
        print('Get up and get ready for work')

Get up and get ready for work
```

INDENTED CODE

Once you type in the colon in the conditional statement, all the lines of code after it must be indented to denote it as the block of code that must be run.

Python is very picky on indentation; it should be the same amount for all the lines of code that are part of the block. It is best to allow the IDLE editor to help with this, instead of typing in your own spaces or tabs.

Nested Conditionals

Often, we may check on another condition after the first one and then decide further. There are no eggs or there is not enough time to make fried eggs for breakfast, so we now check to see if there is time to make oatmeal. We can add an if-else statement inside another one.

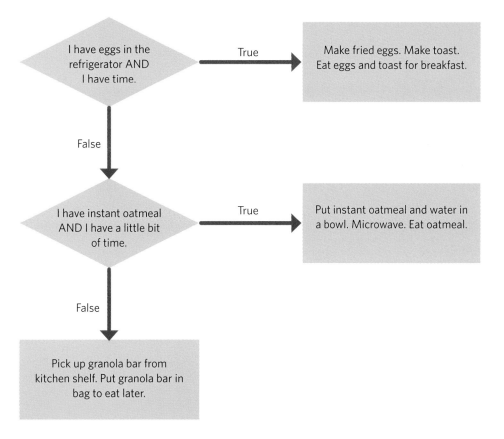

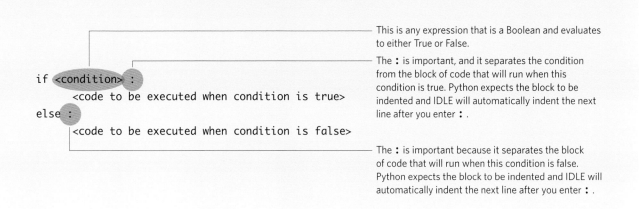

This is any expression that is a Boolean and evaluates to either True or False.

The **:** is important, and it separates the condition from the block of code that will run when this condition is true. Python expects the block to be indented and IDLE will automatically indent the next line after you enter **:** .

The **:** is important because it separates the block of code that will run when this condition is false. Python expects the block to be indented and IDLE will automatically indent the next line after you enter **:** .

Nested Conditionals

Here is a simple number guessing game that you can try by creating a new file called guessNumber.py and entering the following code. In this example, there is an if-else statement inside the else part of the code; if the number entered by the user is not equal to the secret number, then it checks to see if it is lower or higher to give the user the appropriate message.

```python
# Guess the number game
secret_number = 87
n = input('Guess the secret number between 1 and 100 ')
n = int(n)  # convert user input into an integer
if n == secret_number:
    print('You got it!')
else:
    # not equal to secret_number so check if lower or higher
    if n > secret_number:
        print('Your guess was too high')
    else:
        print('Your guess was too low')
print('Thanks for playing')  # this is done at end in all cases
```

Elif Statements

When the problem requires different code blocks for multiple conditions, we can use the **elif** construct in Python instead of multiple nested conditions.

In the example below, a set of code is run for Monday and Wednesday, another is run for Tuesday and Thursday, another is run for Friday, and a final one is run for Saturday and Sunday. Enter this code into a new file called week.py.

```
# day of the week program
day = input('Enter day of the week :')
if day == 'monday' or day == 'wednesday':
    alarm = '7.30am'
    carpool = True
    coding_class = True
    gym = False
elif day == 'tuesday' or day == 'thursday':
    alarm = '7.30am'
    carpool = False
    coding_class = False
    gym = True
elif day == 'friday':
    alarm = '6.30am'
    carpool = True
    coding_class = False
    gym = False
else:
    alarm = 'OFF'
    carpool = False
    coding_class = False
    gym = True
print(alarm, carpool, coding_class, gym)
```

Set the alarm?
Do I have class?
Carpool today?
It depends on the day of the week.

Monday X X
Tuesday X
Wednesday X
Thursday X X
Friday X X X
Saturday X
Sunday X

BOOLEAN OPERATORS REQUIRE BOOLEAN VALUES

A common mistake when using Boolean operators is not using them with Boolean values.

day == 'monday' or 'wednesday' is incorrect because the first part, **day == 'monday'** is Boolean, but **'wednesday'** is a string, not a Boolean. Each part must be a Boolean. The correct way to do this is:

day == 'monday' or day == 'wednesday'

COMPUTERS CAN LOOP BASED ON A CONDITION

Too
high

Too
low

Guess the
number?

83?

27?

Computers can loop (run a set of code repeatedly) as long as a condition remains true. This is called a **conditional loop**.

Unlike the for loop in Chapter 2, which is used to run code a fixed number of times, this kind of loop is used when the exact number of times to run the code is not known. It runs until some condition remains true.

For example, in the guessing game on page 64, we may want to keep playing the game so long as the user has not guessed the number. Instead of specifying a fixed number of tries (a fixed number of times to run the loop), we will let the code run until they guess the number. We use these kind of loops when we do not know how many times it must be repeated. In this example, we do not know how many turns it will take the user to guess the number.

The flowchart at right has a loop—you can see the line going back. The decision box at the top of the loop is the condition to be tested in the conditional loop.

Using a Conditional Loop in Python

In Python, conditional loops can be created using the while statement.

Here is the code for the flowchart. Enter it in a new file called guessNumberVersion2.py.

```
while <condition> :
    <code to be executed when condition is true>
```

This is any expression that is a Boolean and evaluates to either True or False.

The **:** is important because it separates the condition from the block of code that will run when this condition is true. Python expects the block to be indented and IDLE will automatically indent the next line after you enter **:** .

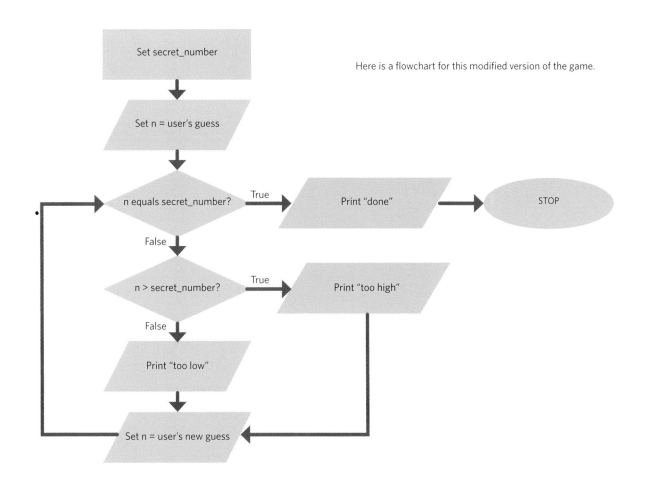

Here is a flowchart for this modified version of the game.

```
# Guess the number game version 2
secret_number = 87
n = input('Guess the secret number between 1 and 100 ')
n = int(n)  # convert user input into an integer

while not (n == secret_number):
    # not equal to secret_number so check if lower or higher
    if n > secret_number:
        print('Your guess was too high')
    else:
        print('Your guess was too low')
    # ask user for another guess
    n = input('Make another guess between 1 and 100 ')
    n = int(n)  # convert user input into an integer
print('You got it !')
```

SAMPLE RUN

Guess the secret number between 1 and 100 89
Your guess was too high
Make another guess between 1 and 100 12
Your guess was too low
Make another guess between 1 and 100 29
Your guess was too low
Make another guess between 1 and 100 99
Your guess was too high
Make another guess between 1 and 100 87
You got it !

Forcing User Input with While Loops

A while loop can be used to force a certain input from the user. For example, if the only choices that should be entered are "yes" and "no", the while loop can run code to keep asking the user to enter input again if their input is something else.

```python
# while loop checks for specific input - a yes or no
choice = input('Enter yes or no :')
while not(choice == 'yes' or choice == 'no'):
    choice = input('Please enter yes or no :')
# end of while loop, code entered here runs when input is valid
```

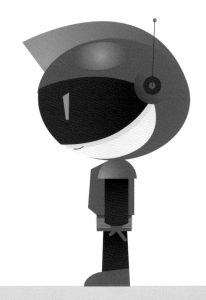

STRUCTURE OF A CONDITIONAL LOOP

All conditional loops are of the form:

Pseudocode

  Set initial condition
  While condition is true :
    Code to be run each time inside loop
    Change condition

In the guessing game example, we set up the initial condition as the first user guess. The condition we test is if the guess is equal to the secret number. The code we run each time is printing too low or too high, and finally, the change condition is allowing the user to enter a new number, so that the condition to be checked will change. What happens if the condition is not changed, if we do not give the user another chance to enter a guess?

PROJECT
CREATING AN
ADVENTURE GAME

This is an example of the popular category of text-based adventure games, also known as **interactive fiction**. The user makes choices and moves through the story, collecting items or answering questions. It is a good opportunity for using conditionals (if statements) and nested conditionals.

Storyline: The user is hiking in the mountains and hears a sound. She gets lost and has to make decisions so that she can get back safely and win the game.

This is a sample—you can customize it to make it your own adventure game. You can extend it with more items, choices, and characters. Creating a more complex adventure game based on this idea is a good way to practice your Python coding skills.

Using a flowchart makes this project easier to plan and code. You will add to the project based on the flowchart at each step. Run the code after each step to make sure it works.

SAMPLE RUN OF THE GAME

```
Welcome to the Santa Cruz Mountain Adventure Game
**************************************************
You are visiting Santa Cruz, California.
You go on an evening hike alone in the mountains.
You can pick one item to take with you -
map(m), flashlight(f), chocolate(c), rope(r), or stick(s) :
What do you choose?: c
You hear a humming sound.
Do you follow the sound? Enter y or n: n
Good idea. You are not taking risks.
You start walking back to the starting point.
You realize you are LOST!
The sound is behind you and is getting louder. You panic!
Do you start running (r) or stop to make a call (c)?: c
The call does not go through.
Do you want to run (r) or try calling again (c)?: c
The call does not go through.
Do you want to run (r) or try calling again (c)?: r
You are running fast. The sound gets really loud.
A woman on an electric scooter comes up behind you.
She asks, "Name my favorite computer programming language.": PYTHON
She says, "Yes, Python is my favorite programming language.
If you have some chocolate, I can help you."
Luckily, you did choose correctly!
You give her the chocolate.
She helps you get home.
CONGRATULATIONS! You got out safely. You won the game.
```

Step 1:
Add an Introduction and Have the User Make a Choice

Start a new file for this project called, for example, AdventureGame.py. Add an introduction to the game using print statements and get the user to pick an item to take on the adventure by using an input.

Then, present the first choice and go different ways using an if statement. See the flowchart below for this step.

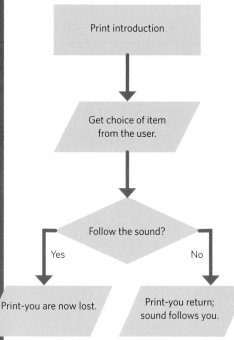

Print introduction

Get choice of item from the user.

Follow the sound?

Yes

No

Print-you are now lost.

Print-you return; sound follows you.

Here is the code for this step.

```
# adventure game
print('Welcome to the Santa Cruz Mountain Adventure Game!')
print('***************************************************')
print('You are visiting Santa Cruz, California.')
print('You go on an evening hike alone in the mountains.')
print('You can pick one item to take with you -  ')
print('map(m), flashlight(f), chocolate(c), rope(r), or stick(s): ')
item = input('What do you choose?: ')
print('You hear a humming sound.')
choice1 = input('Do you follow the sound? Enter y or n: ')
if choice1 == 'y':
    print('You keep moving closer to the sound.')
    print('The sound suddenly stops.')
    print('You are now LOST!  ... ')
    print('You try to call on your phone, but there is no signal!')
else:
    print('Good idea. You are not taking risks. ')
    print('You start walking back to the starting point.')
    print('You realize you are LOST! ')
    print('The sound is behind you and is getting louder. You panic! ')
```

Step 2:
Add a Loop

Now that we have created two different possibilities, we will add more code to extend the story. In this step, we add to the else section (in which the user starts walking back and the sound gets louder).

We give the user a choice to run or call for help, but using a while loop, we only let them proceed if they choose to run.

See the flowchart below for this while loop.

After the else part in Step 1, that is, right after this line of code:

```
print('The sound is behind you and is getting louder. You panic! ')
```

Add the following code:

```
action = input('Do you start running (r), stop to make a call (c)?: ')
while action == 'c':
    print('The call does not go through')
    action = input('Do you want to run (r), or try calling again (c)?: ')
print('You are running fast. The sound gets really loud')
```

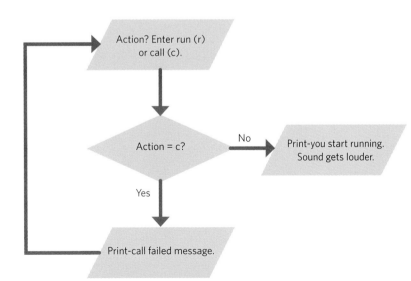

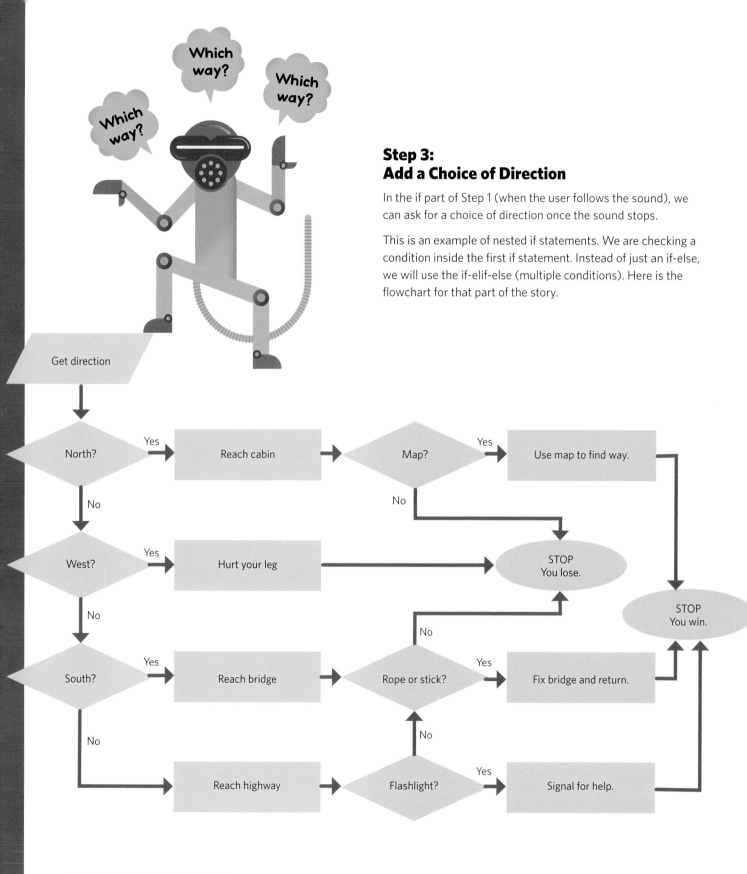

Step 3:
Add a Choice of Direction

In the if part of Step 1 (when the user follows the sound), we can ask for a choice of direction once the sound stops.

This is an example of nested if statements. We are checking a condition inside the first if statement. Instead of just an if-else, we will use the if-elif-else (multiple conditions). Here is the flowchart for that part of the story.

After the if part in Step 1, that is, right after this line of code:

```
print('You try to call on your phone, there is no signal!')
```

Add the following code:

```
direction = input('Which direction do you go? north, south, east, or west: ')
if direction == 'north':
    print('You reach an abandoned cabin.')
    if item == 'm':
        print('You use the map and find your way home.')
        print('CONGRATULATIONS! You won the game. ')
    else:
        print('If you had a map, you could find your way from here.')
        print('---You are still lost. You lost the game.---')
elif direction == 'south':
    print('You reach a river with a broken bridge.')
    if item == 'r' or item == 's':
        print('You chose an item that can fix the bridge.')
        print('You fix the bridge, cross over, and find your way home')
        print('CONGRATULATIONS! You won the game.')
    else:
        print('If you had a rope or a stick, you could fix the bridge.')
        print('---You are still lost. You lost the game.---')
elif direction == 'west':
    print('You are walking and trip over a fallen log.')
    print('You have hurt your foot. You sit down and wait for help.')
    print('This could be a long time. You are still lost.')
    print('---You lost the game.---')
else:
    print('You reach the side of the highway. It is dark.')
    if item == 'f':
        print('You use the flashlight to signal.')
        print('A car stops and gives you a ride home.')
        print('CONGRATULATIONS! You got out safely. You won the game.')
    else:
        print('If you had a flashlight, you could signal for help.')
        print('---You are still lost. You lost the game.--')
```

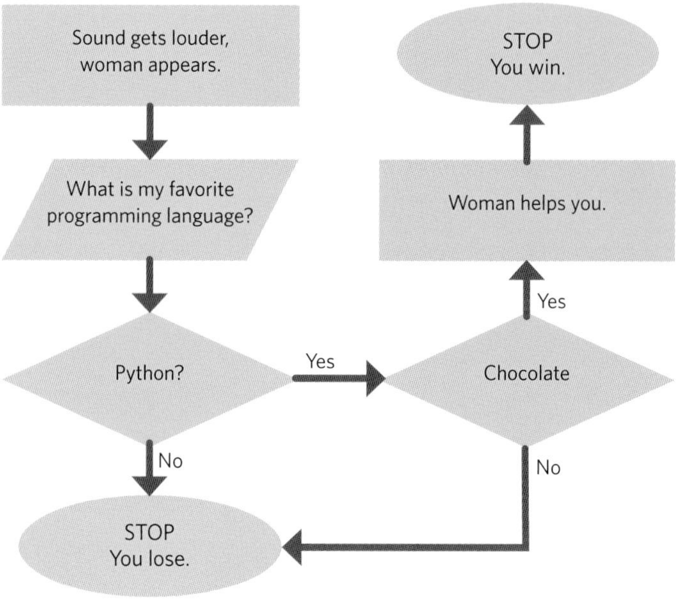

Step 4:
Make the User Answer a Question to Determine the Next Action

Add a puzzle or quiz question that the user must answer correctly to determine the next action. Add this after the user is running fast, after the code in Step 2.

After this while loop, when you are running fast, that is, after the line:

```
print('You are running fast and then the sound gets really loud')
```

Add this code:

```
print('A woman on an electric scooter comes up behind you.')
answer = input('She says, "Name my favorite computer programming language.": ')
if answer == 'python':
    print('She says, "Yes, Python is my favorite programming language."')
    print('"If you have some chocolate, I can help you."')
    if item == 'c':
        print('Luckily you did choose correctly!')
        print('You give her the chocolate.')
        print('She helps you get home.')
        print('CONGRATULATIONS! You got out safely. You won the game.')
    else:
        print('You should have chosen that chocolate!')
        print('She rides away, leaving you alone and lost.')
        print('You lost the game.')
else:
    print('She did not like your answer.')
    print('She rides away, leaving you lost!')
    print('You lost the game.')
```

The flowchart on the right shows:

- Sound gets louder, woman appears.
- ↓
- What is my favorite programming language?
- ↓
- Python? — No → STOP You lose.
- Python? — Yes → Chocolate
- Chocolate — No → STOP You lose.
- Chocolate — Yes → Woman helps you.
- ↑
- STOP You win.

Step 5:
Improve User Input and Add Error Checking

We can make some improvements to the game now that we have something working.

We can improve the step at which the user must type in "python" by allowing them to type in the answer using uppercase, lowercase, or a combination—that is, "Python", "python," or "PYTHON."

One way to do this is to check for each possible user input. So we can change this part:

```
if answer == 'python':
```

to:

```
if answer == 'python' or answer == 'Python' or answer == 'PYTHON':
```

This will work but seems repetitive. Instead, you can convert the user's response to lowercase and just check that. Luckily, this is easy to do in Python. You can use the **lower** method on any string to convert it to lowercase, as follows:

```
if answer.lower() == 'python':
```

We can also add some basic error checking. Using what we learned in the previous section, we can add a while loop and force the user to retry if they do not type in the correct answer. When we ask the user to make the first choice between y and n, we can check that they actually type one of them. The Boolean condition **(choice1 == 'y' or choice1 == 'n')** must be true if the input is valid. We will retry if this condition is not true, so we use **not (choice1 == 'y' or choice1 == 'n')** at the start of the while loop. The new code for this section is as follows:

```
choice1 = input('Do you follow the sound? Enter y or n: ')
while not (choice1 == 'y' or choice1 == 'n'):
    choice1 = input('That is an invalid input. Enter y or n: ')
```

CODING TIP

The best way to work on any coding project is to make incremental steps; do not write in too much code at a time. Once a piece is working, you can always go back and improve something or change it to run better.

MANIPULATING TEXT

In addition to lower() function, there are several other powerful ways to manipulate text (strings) in Python. One way to find them is to type in the string and a '.' and wait in the Python IDLE editor; it autofills to tell you what is possible. Take a look at the What's Next section at the end of this book for more information on how to do this.

Step 6:
Add Pauses in the Story

To make the game run better, you can slow down the output by inserting a pause. This allows the user to read and makes it more dramatic. For example, in the beginning of the story, just before you tell the user they are lost, you can stop for few seconds before you continue.

To insert this pause, use the sleep function, which is part of another Python module—the time module. To use a pause in your code, insert the following on top of your file:

```
import time
```

Then, at any place you want to pause, enter the following code. The number in parentheses is the number of seconds. For a 3-second pause, use:

```
time.sleep(3)
```

Try changing the code in Step 1 to:

```
if choice1 == 'y':
    print('You keep moving closer to the sound.')
    print('The sound suddenly stops.')
    time.sleep(3)  # add a 3 second pause here for user to read
    print('You are now LOST!  ... ')
    time.sleep(3)  # add a 3 second dramatic pause here
    print('You try to call on your phone, there is no signal!')
```

Step 7:
Add More to Make the Game Better

There are many ways you can make this game much better. Here are a few:

❶ Change the actual text of the story to a better story.

❷ Change or add more items to choose in the beginning.

❸ Change or add more questions asked by the woman and the resulting actions.

❹ Add more puzzles in the form of questions and items to be collected.

❺ Add more error checking; check if all input is valid.

❻ Add more ways for the user to respond; instead of just y or n, maybe allow yes and no.

❼ Add an energy variable that changes as you move through various levels.

❽ Add more pauses, using the sleep function, to make the game run better.

❾ Add some text graphics to make the output look better.

Adding more complexity and decision-making to the story will make it better. Use as many ideas as possible to expand your game.

All you need is your creativity and some more Python code!

EXPERIMENT AND EXTEND

Experiment 1:
Password Checker

Create a password checking program that lets the user keep trying until they get it correct. Use any password to test your program.

Pseudocode

Get password from user
While password is not correct
    Print incorrect
    Get password from user
Print Correct

Sample Run

```
Enter the password :python17
Sorry that is incorrect
Enter password again :lab28!
Sorry that is incorrect
Enter password again :secret987
Success: You are correct
```

Experiment 2 :
Dog or Cat to Human Age Calculator

Many people multiply the age of a dog by 7 to get the equivalent age in human years. A more accurate calculation for the age of dogs and cats in human years is as follows.

Dogs:

- 1st dog year = 12 human years
- 2nd dog year = 24 human years
- Add four years for every year after that.

So a 6 year old dog would be 40 in human years.

Cats:

- 1st cat year = 15 human years
- 2nd cat year = 24 human years
- Add four years for every year after that.

So a 4 year old cat would be 32 in human years.

Using this information, write a program that asks the user if the animal is a dog or cat, along with its current age, and prints out age of the animal in human years.

Sample Run

```
Enter dog or cat: cat
Enter age of animal: 4
Human age of cat is 32
```

Experiment 3:
Quiz Game

Create a program that asks the user a fixed number of questions on any topic and then gives them a score depending on how many are correct. Use a list for the questions and a list for the corresponding answers.

Pseudocode

Set score to 0
Set n to number of questions in list
Repeat n times the following
    Print question from list
    Get answer from user
    if answer is correct
        Print Correct
        Increase score by 1
    else
        Print Incorrect
        Print the correct answer
Print score.

Sample Run with Two Questions

```
What is the capital of Peru: Lima
You are correct
Which is the longest river: Nile
You are incorrect
The correct answer is Amazon
Your score is 1
```

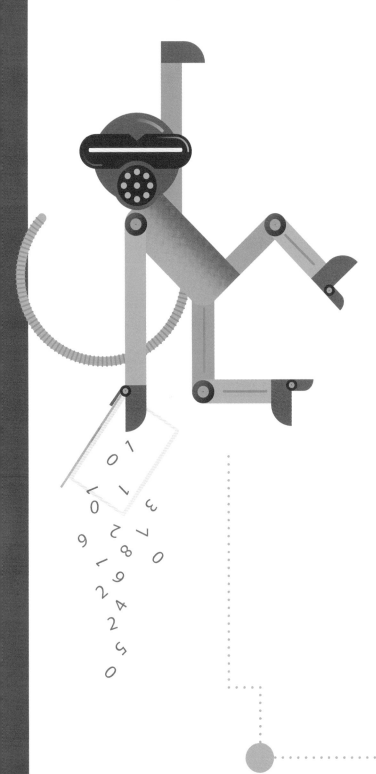

Experiment 4:
Count by 2s, 3s, or
Multiples of Any Number

Print numbers starting from 0 in multiples of the number the user selects. For example, if the user wants to count by 7s, then print 0, 7, 14, 21, 28, and so on until the user enters quit.

Pseudocode

Get count by from user

Set n to 0

Get user choice - quit or not

While user choice is not quit do the following

    Print n

    Increase n by count by

    Get user choice - quit or not

SAMPLE RUN

```
Enter number you want to count by :7
Enter return to continue or q to quit:
0
Enter return to continue or q to quit:
7
Enter return to continue or q to quit:
14
Enter return to continue or q to quit:
21
Enter return to continue or q to quit:
28
Enter return to continue or q to quit:
35
Enter return to continue or q to quit:
42
Enter return to continue or q to quit:q
```

Experiment 5:
Extend the Chatbot

Use conditional statements to make the chatbot from Chapter 1 better.

For example, reply with an appropriate response to how the user is feeling, depending on whether the user is happy, sad, bored, or the like.

Sample Run

```
How are you feeling today?: sad
Sorry to hear you are sad. Why are you feeling
this way? :
```

Generate poems that surprise your friends.

Build smart strategies for your computer games.

Create art that changes each time the program runs.

4

Use your creativity and create your own games of chance.

Build your own functions to reuse code in powerful ways.

CREATE YOUR OWN DICE GAMES

Challenge your friends to your custom word games.

BIG IDEA
CREATING
YOUR OWN FUNCTIONS

We have already seen several built-in Python functions, including print, input, and of course, the turtle functions. Now, we will learn how to make our own functions.

Functions allows us to name a block of code and then reuse it later by using the name.

A simple example is the code we wrote in Chapter 2 for creating a square with the turtle. If we name the code *square*, we (or anyone who uses our code) can create a square at any time, by just calling it by name.

There are two parts to using your own functions:

❶ **Defining the function**. Think of this as teaching the computer a new word. In the example above, we teach the computer how to respond to the word *square* by making a square.

❷ **Calling the function**. Think of this as using the new word that you have made.

In addition to making reusing code easier, functions help us organize our code and share it with others.

How Functions Are Used in Python

Functions are created in Python using the keyword *def*, the name of function, any **parameters**—information the function takes—within parentheses, and then a colon to separate the block of code that must be indented below it. Again, IDLE will auto-indent any line after entering **:** .

Let us look at the example of creating a square using the turtle. We saw the following code in Chapter 2:

```
import turtle
shelly = turtle.Turtle()

for i in range(4):
    shelly.forward(100)
    shelly.left(90)
```

We can take the code that draws the square and give it the name *square* using the keyword *def*. We can then call this function a few times by using square() to make squares.

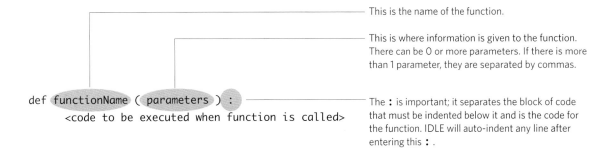

This is the name of the function.

This is where information is given to the function. There can be 0 or more parameters. If there is more than 1 parameter, they are separated by commas.

The **:** is important; it separates the block of code that must be indented below it and is the code for the function. IDLE will auto-indent any line after entering this **:** .

Try this by creating a new file called myfunctions1.py and the code below:

```
# my functions

import turtle
shelly = turtle.Turtle()

# square function creates square of size 100
def square():
    for i in range(4):
        shelly.forward(100)  # each side of square is 100
        shelly.left(90)

square()  # calling the function
shelly.forward(100)  # move forward
square()  # make another square by calling the function
shelly.forward(100)  # move forward
square()  # make another square by calling the function again
```

As you can see in the code above, we do not write out the lines of code to make the three squares each time. The code is more organized and easier to read, and we can reuse the code for the square easily multiple times.

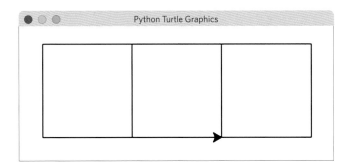

Functions with Parameters

In the square function on the last page, we had no parameters; it did not take any information. This always makes a square of size 100. We can change that by adding a size as a parameter so that it is more flexible and can make squares of any size.

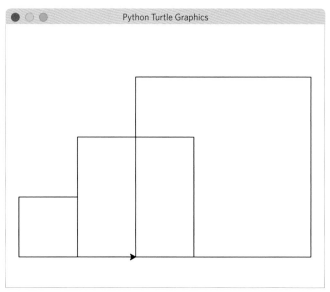

Copy the code from the previous project into a new file called myfunctions2.py and change the square function to use a size as a parameter. See the code below. The name of the parameter in this example is **s**, but you can pick any name. Inside the code for the function, **s** is used instead of a fixed number 100, so it draws a square on any size that is given to it as a parameter.

To use the square, you must now enter the size needed as a parameter. So square(100) makes a square of size 100; square(200) makes a square of size 200.

Parameters make the square function more flexible and powerful because the same code can be used in many ways.

```
# my functions with parameters

import turtle
shelly = turtle.Turtle()

# square function creates square of ANY size
def square(s):
    for i in range(4):
        shelly.forward(s)  # each side of square is variable s
        shelly.left(90)

square(100)  # calling the function for square of size 100
shelly.forward(100)  # move forward
square(200)  # calling the function for square of size 200
shelly.forward(100)  # move forward
square(300)  # calling the function for square of size 300
```

The square function can be used anywhere you use a Python function. For example, you can use square function inside a for loop. What does the following make?

```
for i in range(25):
    square(i)
    shelly.forward(i)
```

Functions with Return Values

Sometimes, a function returns something that the rest of the code can use.

For example, we can create a function that takes a list of scores and returns their average. In a new file called myfunctions3.py, enter and run the following:

```python
# functions that return values
# define a function that finds average of a list
def average(myList):
    total = sum(myList)  # use the sum function in Python lists
    average = total / len(myList)  # len gives number of items
    return average

# use the function
scores = [7, 23, 56, 89]
averageScore = average(scores)
print('The average of the scores is', averageScore)
```

Here is another example in which the function returns a list of cards made from two lists. This can be used to create a card game—see the Experiment and Extend section.

```python
suits = ['Clubs', 'Hearts', 'Diamonds', 'Spades']
cardno = ['2', '3', '4', '5', '6', '7', '8', '9', '10', 'J', 'Q', \
'K', 'A']

def make_cards():
    cards = []  # start with empty list and add cards
    for s in suits:
        for i in cardno:  # for each card number in each suit
            cards.append(i + '-' + s)
    return cards
my_cards = make_cards()
print(my_cards)
```

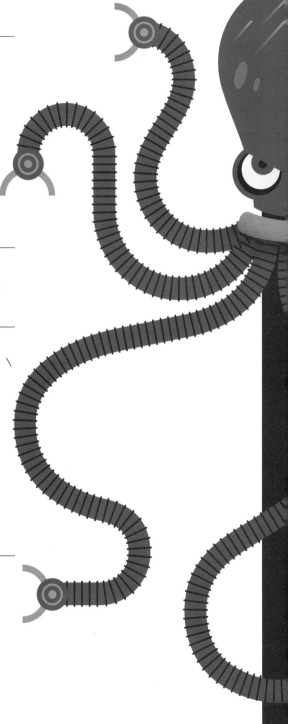

COMPUTERS CAN PICK ITEMS AT RANDOM

When we create games, we often want to add an element of chance. Instead of deciding on an item, we want the computer to pick something at random.

For example, to improve the number guessing game from Chapter 3, we may want the computer to pick a number between 1 and 100 at random, instead of writing it in our code. This way, it is different each time we run the program and even the programmer does not have the correct answer.

In the case of the adventure game in Chapter 3, we may want a variation in which the computer picks which is the lucky item that is needed in the last stage of the game. Instead of deciding on using "chocolate" as the item needed at the final stage, let the computer pick an item at random so that the game ends differently with each run.

Think of this as a computer picking items from a bag at random.

Picking Items at Random in Python

In Python, we can select random items by using the random module. So on top of your code, use:

```
import random
```

To select a number at random between a start range and an end range, use: **random.randint(start of range, end of range)**.

So, to pick a number between 1 and 100, use:

```
random.randint(1,100)
```

To select an item at random from a list called listname, use **random.choice(listname)**.

```
>>> fruit = ['apples', 'cherries', 'bananas', 'strawberries']
>>> random.choice(fruit)
```

BIG IDEA
LOOPING THROUGH A LIST OR A STRING

Computers are very good at looping—repeating things again and again either a fixed number of times, while a condition is true, or for each item in a list or string.

For any list of items (for example, names, phone numbers, or scores), we often want to create a loop in which the computer goes through the list and executes a fixed amount of code for each item.

We can think of text as a list of characters, and we can loop through the text and do something with each character. This is especially useful in manipulating information inputted by the user or in a text-based project such as a word game.

hello Kyle

hello Trisha

hello Nico

TRISHA

KYLE

NICO

NAMES

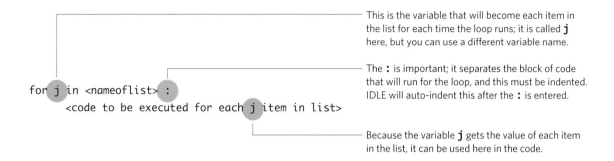

for j in <nameoflist> :
    <code to be executed for each j item in list>

This is the variable that will become each item in the list for each time the loop runs; it is called **j** here, but you can use a different variable name.

The **:** is important; it separates the block of code that will run for the loop, and this must be indented. IDLE will auto-indent this after the **:** is entered.

Because the variable **j** gets the value of each item in the list, it can be used here in the code.

Looping Through a List or String in Python

In Chapter 2, we saw how Python can loop through a fixed number of times. For example, to say hello ten times, we can use:

```
for i in range(10):
  print('Hello')
```

The **range (10)** causes Python to create an internal list of numbers from 0 to 9 that it uses to loop through.

We can use this same idea for any list that we use.

For example:

```
>>> names = ['alex', 'bob', 'sue', 'dave', 'emily']
>>> for i in names:
        print('Welcome to the class', i)
```

The variable **i** is equal to each item in the list in turn. So i = alex, then i = bob, and so on as it executes the code. Try the code in the Python shell. It should give the following:

```
Welcome to the class alex
Welcome to the class bob
Welcome to the class sue
Welcome to the class dave
Welcome to the class emily
```

Strings work in a similar way: the loop is per character in the string. Here is an example.

```
>>> s = 'Python'
>>> for i in s:
        print(i)
```

```
P
y
t
h
o
n
```

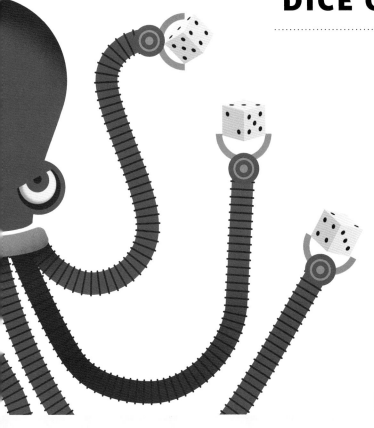

PROJECT
CREATING YOUR OWN
DICE GAME

Let us make a dice game in which the computer and the user take turns rolling a fixed number of dice to see who can get the highest total. Each gets one chance to roll again and can decide which of the dice rolled must be held or rerolled.

In the sample run below, the game is for six dice. The user gets a roll of 4, 6, 5, 6, 2, and 5 and decides to hold all except the 2. They enter choices using "-" to hold and "r" to roll again. After the user gets a new roll, the computer rolls, following a strategy in which anything below 5 must be rerolled. In this game, the computer wins.

We will look at how the computer could use different strategies to decide on what to hold and what to roll.

We can also change the objective of the game from highest total to lowest total or the highest number of 6s rolled or something else.

Because the computer and the user make similar moves, we will use functions where possible to reuse the code.

SAMPLE RUN OF THE DICE GAME

```
Enter number of dice:6
Ready to start? Hit any key to continue
User first roll:  [4, 6, 5, 6, 2, 5]
Enter - to hold or r to roll again :----r-
Rolling again ...
User new Roll: [4, 6, 5, 6, 3, 5]
Computers turn
Computer first roll:  [1, 6, 5, 5, 4, 6]
Computer is thinking ...
Computer Choice:  r---r-
Rolling again ...
Computer new Roll:  [5, 6, 5, 5, 6, 6]
Computer total 33
User total 29
Computer wins
```

ARTIFICIAL INTELLIGENCE IN GAMES

Many games use some amount of artificial intelligence (AI), usually to turn the computer into an interesting opponent to the human player. The amount of artificial intelligence varies based on the complexity of the game. It could be as simple as programming a computer to play a dice game like the one in this chapter or as complicated as creating a program to play a complex game such as chess with a human champion. Some games have AI that uses strategies that are created based on data gathered from previous runs of the game—this is the machine-learning part of AI.

Step 1:
Have the User Select the Number of Dice

Create a new file called Dicegame.py and add a comment on top. Ask the user for the number of dice to be used in this game and store it in a variable called **number_dice**. Before starting the game, ask the user to hit a key when they are ready for the game.

```
# dice game

# step1 in main program area - start game
number_dice = input('Enter number of dice:')
number_dice = int(number_dice)
ready = input('Ready to start? Hit any key to continue')
```

Run the above program and make sure it works.

CHOOSING GOOD FUNCTION NAMES

The names of the function must not have spaces or special characters. You can use any name, but picking one that describes what the function does is good programming practice since it makes the code easy to read and change later. So, while you can name the code that decides on the winner with a function called Icecream, it is best to use something like findwinner, or to make it more readable, we can use find_winner or FindWinner. Most Python programmers use lower case with "_" where needed for readability, so in this book we will use names like find_winner for our functions.

Step 2:
Create a Function to Roll the Dice

The dice rolled will be represented by a list of numbers, where each number is the value of the dice. For example, if there are 6 dice, a dice roll of 3, 4, 5, 6, 6, 1 can be represented by the list [3,4,5,6,6,1]. For the number of dice needed, we must use **random.randint(1,6)** to generate a number between 1 and 6 and add it to the list. We can start with an empty list as a variable called **dice** (the empty list is indicated by [], which is the open [followed by the closed]) and then add to this list by appending random numbers using **dice.append(random.randint(1,6))**. We will do this inside a for loop as many times as the number of dice in the game (using the previous variable **number_dice**).

In order to use randomness in the game, we must of course import the random module so we can use the random function.

To create a list for the computer or the user, we will use a function that takes the number of dice as a parameter and then returns this dice list. This is the code to be added to the top of the file (it will be above the code in Step 1).

```
import random
def roll_dice(n):
    dice = []   # start with empty list of dice
    # add random numbers between 1 to 6 to the list
    for i in range(n):
        dice.append(random.randint(1,6))
    return dice
```

We can then use the above function for the user and for the computer. Add this below the code entered in Step 1:

```
# step 2 in main program area - roll dice
# User turn to roll
user_rolls = roll_dice(number_dice)
print('User first roll: ', user_rolls)
# Computer's turn to roll
print('Computers turn ')
computer_rolls = roll_dice(number_dice)
print('Computer first roll: ', computer_rolls)
```

DEFINE YOUR FUNCTIONS BEFORE YOU USE THEM

Functions must be defined before they are used. It is best to define these at the top of the file and clearly mark the main code area that uses these function with a comment below.

Also import of any modules must be done before anything else and is best done on top. So any program file will be of the type:

```
import …
def function1():
...
def function2():
...
# main program code
```

Run the program, and you should have the beginning part working.

Sample Run
```
Enter number of dice:6
Ready to start? Hit any key to continue
User first roll:  [6, 3, 6, 4, 2, 3]
Computers turn
Computer first roll:  [5, 6, 4, 4, 3, 5]
```

Step 3:
Decide the Winner

Before adding the rest of the game, let's write the function that decides on the winner. This function takes the lists of dice for the user and the computer, gets the sum of the each, and prints out who wins or if it is a tie.

The sum function for lists makes finding the sum of a list of numbers easy. Once we have the total for the computer and the user, we can use a conditional statement to determine and print the winner. Add this function below the function **roll_dice**.

```python
def find_winner(cdice_list, udice_list):
    computer_total = sum(cdice_list)
    user_total = sum(udice_list)
    print('Computer total', computer_total)
    print('User total',user_total )
    if user_total > computer_total:
        print('User wins')
    elif user_total < computer_total:
        print('Computer wins')
    else:
        print('It is a tie!')
```

Now, call this function just after the code in Step 2 in the main program area using:

```python
# final line in code - deciding who wins
find_winner(computer_rolls,user_rolls)
```

Run the program to see if it works.

Sample Run

```
Enter number of dice:6
Ready to start? Hit any key to continue
User first roll:  [4, 4, 1, 4, 5, 3]
Computers turn
Computer first roll:  [1, 5, 2, 6, 2, 4]
Computer total 20
User total 21
User wins
```

Step 4:
Ask the User to Hold or Roll Again

We can now ask the user if they want to hold or roll each of the dice after their initial roll. We will use a string for this user input; the user enters a **-** to hold and **r** to roll. We can loop through this user input to decide which dice must be rerolled to recalculate the list.

We will also use a while loop to do some error checking and make sure the user enters the correct number of holds and rolls and force them to reenter data if necessary. This error checking is important so the rest of the game works.

Here is the code to be added after the code for the user rolls, just before the computer rolls.

```
# step 4 - get user choices
user_choices = input("Enter - to hold or r to \
roll again :")
# check length of user input
while len(user_choices) != number_dice:
    print('You must enter', number_dice, \
'choices')
    user_choices = input("Enter - to hold or r \
to roll again :")
```

Step 5:
Create a Function that Rerolls

Now that we have the user choices as a string, we can use that string and the original dice roll, which was stored as a list, to create a new version of the list. Because we will do this for both the user and the computer, we will again use a function. This function needs to know which list is to be modified and which set of choices is being used to modify the list. We must also add **import time** at the top to add the pause in the game here. Add this function toward the top of the file after the other functions.

```
def roll_again(choices, dice_list):
    print('Rolling again ...')
    time.sleep(3)
    for i in range(len(choices)):
        if choices[i] == 'r':
            dice_list[i] = random.randint(1,6)
    time.sleep(3)
```

Now that we have a roll again function, call this function after the user makes their choices, as follows:

```
# step 5 - roll again based on user choices
roll_again(user_choices, user_rolls)
print('Player new Roll: ', user_rolls)
```

Run the program. The user can now decide what to hold and what to reroll, and this determines the next roll.

Sample Run

```
Enter number of dice:6
Ready to start? Hit any key to continue
User first roll:  [5, 3, 1, 1, 4, 5]
Enter - to hold or r to roll again :--rr--
Rolling again ...
Player new Roll:  [5, 3, 4, 1, 4, 5]
Computers turn
Computer first roll:  [4, 4, 2, 3, 5, 4]
Computer total 22
User total 22
It is a tie!
```

Step 6:
Use a Strategy to Determine the Computer's Choices

Now that the user's choices have been made and the dice have been rerolled, we must allow the computer to make its choice on what dice to hold and what to roll again. We can use different strategies to do this. Here are two possibilities:

Strategy 1: Roll everything, so the choice string is just a series of *rs*.

Strategy 2: Roll only if the number is less than 5; we will need to use an if-else statement here.

We can implement each strategy using a function that gives the choices as a string. You can add one or both to the top of your file. A new string is created called **choices** and returned from the function.

```python
def computer_strategy1(n):
    # create computer choices : roll everything again
    print('Computer is thinking ...')
    time.sleep(3)
    choices = ''  # start with an empty list of choices
    for i in range(n):
        choices = choices + 'r'
    return choices


def computer_strategy2(n):
    # create computer choices: roll if < 5
    print('Computer is thinking ...')
    time.sleep(3)
    choices = ''  # start with an empty list of choices
    for i in range(n):
        if computer_rolls[i] < 5:
            choices = choices + 'r'
        else:
            choices = choices + '-'
    return choices
```

Now, just after the computer rolls, call one of these strategies to create a new list of choices and use it in the **roll_again** function as follows. Add this code just before the call to **find_winner**, which you added in Step 3. Remember, finding the winner is the last line in the project. Check the complete project code online (see page 138) to make sure you have added the code in the right order.

```
# step 6
# decide on what choice  - using one of the strategy functions
computer_choices = computer_strategy2(number_dice)
print('Computer Choice: ', computer_choices)
# Computer rolls again using the choices it made
roll_again(computer_choices, computer_rolls)
print('Computer new Roll: ', computer_rolls)
```

How Can You Make This Game Better?

There are many ways to improve this game.

- Allow two or three rerolls, to allow the user or computer to improve the final score.
- Run the entire game inside a loop, to allow three rounds of the game to determine a final winner.
- Change the winning objective—get the lowest score, the maximum number of sixes, or something else.
- Is < 5 the best strategy to decide on a reroll? Modify the code for the strategy or add more strategies and/or give the user a choice of difficulty level to determine which strategy will be used by the computer.
- Add some better formatting and/or ASCII art to make the text-based game look better.

This dice game is yours. You can customize it and make it unique using your creativity and some Python code.

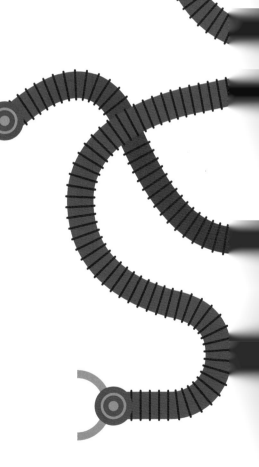

EXPERIMENT AND EXTEND

Experiment 1:
Create Abstract Art

Use random colors, randomly sized circles, and randomly sized squares to create abstract art that is different each time you run the program.

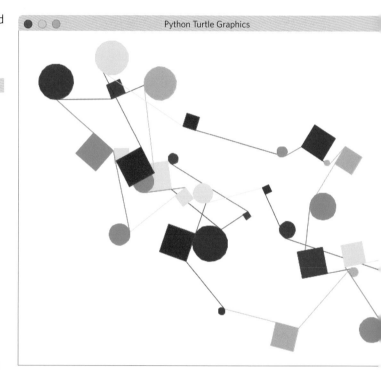

Pseudocode

Import turtle module

Import random module

Create turtle

Create a list of colors using a list like in chapter 2

Do the following 100 times

   Move turtle forward random amount between 0 and 360

   Start filling color

   Set up random fill color

   Set size to random amount between 10 and 50

   Draw square using square function with size

   End filling color of square

   Move turtle forward random amount between 20 and 100

   Turn turtle a random number between 0 and 360

   Start filling color

   Set up random fill color

   Draw a circle with random amount between 5 and 30

   End filling color of circle

Experiment 2:
Create Changing Landscapes

Use the following house function—which is based off the experiment on page 51—with different sizes and colors, to create several random houses in a landscape that changes each time the program is run.

Pseudocode

Import turtle module

Import random module

Create turtle

Create a list of colors

Copy the function code from below

Set background color to blue

Do the following 10 times

    Set x to a random between -200 and 200

    Set y to a random between -200 and 200

    Set wall_color to random color from list

    Set roof_color to random color from list

    Call function house with parameters x, y, wall_color, roof_color

```python
def house(x, y, wallColor, roofColor):
    shelly.penup()  # Lift pen before moving to new location
    shelly.goto(x,y)  # move turtle to position
    shelly.setheading(0)  # set turtle to point to the right
    shelly.pendown()  # put pen down and get ready to draw
    shelly.begin_fill()
    shelly.color(wallColor)  # set color and make square
    for i in range(4):
        shelly.right(90)
        shelly.forward(30)
    shelly.end_fill()
    shelly.backward(35)  # go back and get ready for roof
    shelly.begin_fill()  # start fill of color for roof
    shelly.color(roofColor)
    shelly.left(60)
    shelly.forward(40)
    shelly.right(120)
    shelly.forward(40)
    shelly.right(120)
    shelly.forward(40)
    shelly.end_fill()  # end fill of color for roof
```

Experiment 3: Generate Poems

Set up lists of words—adjectives, verbs, and the like—and generate a poem. For an extra challenge, try and create a poem of a particular type, such as a haiku or a limerick, by choosing words for the list accordingly. Let the user decide if they want another poem or to quit, to allow them to get one or more poems.

Sample Run

```
Enter any key for another poem or enter q to quit
------------------------------
There once was a girl called Serena
who wanted to be a ballerina.
She played on a flat
and made friends with a cat,
And ended up lost in Pensylvina.
------------------------------
Enter any key for another poem or enter q to quit
------------------------------
There once was a girl called Tymina
who wanted to be a ballerina.
She danced on a hat
and made friends with a rat,
And ended up lost in Transelina.
------------------------------
Enter any key for another poem or enter q to quit q
```

Experiment 4: Create a Card Game

Create a card game in which the user and the computer pick from a set of cards and the higher card wins. Add your own rules on scoring and how long the game runs. Use code from the Big Idea section on creating a deck of cards as a list. Use **random.choice(list)** to get a card at random from the list. To remove an item from the deck, use **my_cards. remove(card)** where **my_cards** is the list returned from the **make_cards** function.

Use the function **find_card_order** below to determine if one card is higher. (Note that this function assumes you are using the code from the Big Idea section on creating a card deck.) This function returns same, lower, or higher depending on whether the first card is the same, lower, or higher than the second card. If the cards are not identical, it finds the first part of the card name (which is the card number), then the order in the list of card numbers, and then returns higher or lower based on this position.

```
def find_card_order(card1, card2):
    if card1 == card2:
        return 'same'  # picked the same card
    cpos1 = card1[0: card1.find('-')]
    cpos2 = card2[0: card2.find('-')]
    order1 = cardno.index(cpos1)
    order2 = cardno.index(cpos2)
    if order1 > order2:
        return 'higher'
    elif order1 < order2:
        return 'lower'
    else:  # same cardno but not same suit
        return 'same'
```

Experiment 5:
Create an Unscramble Word Game

Create an unscramble word game in which the computer gives the user a scrambled word from a list and the user guesses the word. You can add your own rules on scoring, if the user can quit at any point or must play all the words, and if there are hints. Use the following function to scramble the word:

```python
def scramble(w):
    # turn string into list letters
    letters = list(w)
    random.shuffle(letters)
    # build scramble_word using letters
    scramble_word = ''
    for i in letters:
        scramble_word = scramble_word + i
    return scramble_word
```

python!

Other Experiments

Try to make:

- A fortune teller
- Rock, Paper, Scissors
- A countdown timer that allows the user to enter the timer amount in number of seconds and then counts down from that number to 0

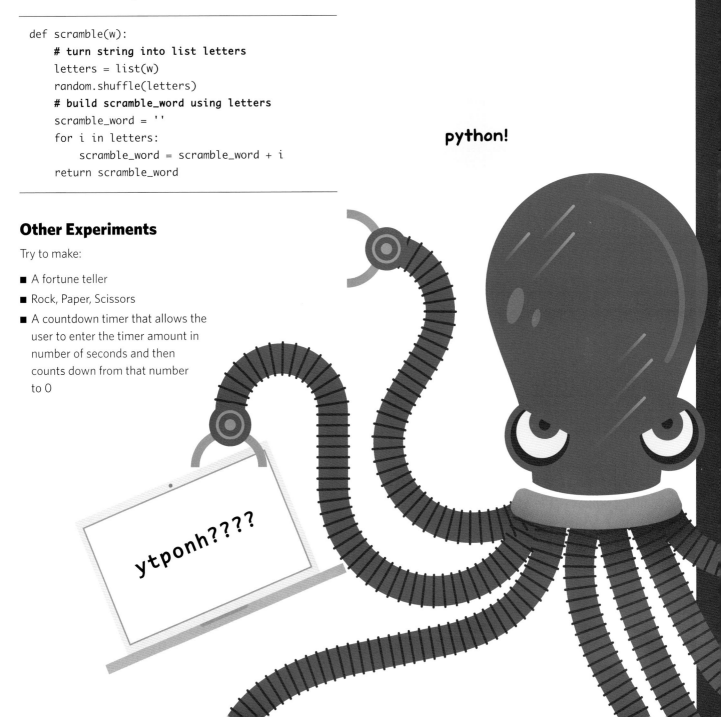

5

Create apps that have windows, buttons, images, and more.

Use your creativity to create your own special arcade games.

Write code to handle keyboard and mouse controls.

CREATE YOUR OWN APPS AND GAMES

Give a graphical interface to all your coding projects.

BIG IDEA
GRAPHICAL USER INTERFACES (GUI)

PRESS HERE

Graphical User Interfaces, more popularly called **GUI** (pronounced goo-ee), allow users to interact with the computer using graphical elements such as icons instead of text-based commands that are typed. Most games and applications (apps) on your computer or phone use GUI; you click on icons, buttons, or menus.

The games in Chapters 3 and 4 allowed only text-based input from the user. In this chapter, we learn how to use GUI in our games and apps.

Creating GUI in Python

Python has a standard module for creating GUI called Tkinter. Tkinter is cross-platform, which means that the Python code used to build an application can be run on any platform (PC, Mac, Linux, etc). Because Tkinter is a module, any Python program using it must import it. This must be added at the top of the code.

```
from tkinter import *
```

EVENT-DRIVEN PROGRAMMING

GUI programs are different from the other programs in that they have to respond to external events—for example, a user clicking on a button, pressing a key, or resizing a window. This type of programming is called **event-driven programming**. GUI programs have a **main event loop** that listens for events and then calls on code (functions) to handle these events; these type of functions are called **event handlers**.

TKINTER IMPORT

The import code here is different than what we used for the turtle module in Chapter 2 or the random module in Chapter 4. This way of importing allows us to use all the functions in the Tkinter module without prefixing it with the word **tkinter**.

GUI EVENT LOOP

Because a program that uses GUI may change any part of the screen and be able to react to any events, it must be constantly checking to see if the screen must be updated and refreshed. It must also listen to the events (keyboard controls or mouse clicks) and handle them by calling the event handlers.

GUI Event Loops in Python

The Tkinter module has a GUI event loop called the **main loop**, and it should be the last line of code in any GUI project. It loops continuously, listening and handling events and updating the screen until the user closes the window (or the program calls a window destroy function). Assuming the name of the variable for the window is `window`, this is the last line that must be added.

```
window.mainloop()
```

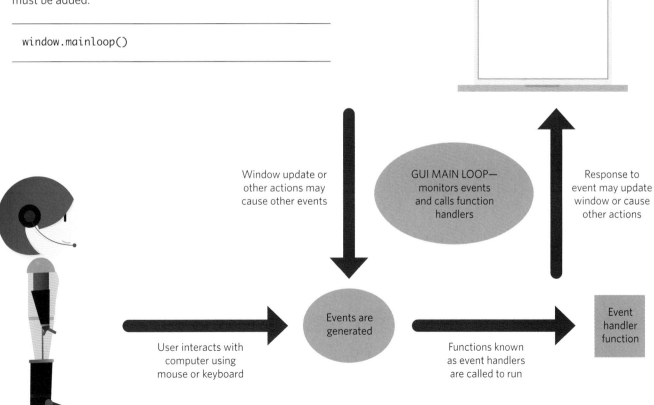

Window update or other actions may cause other events

GUI MAIN LOOP— monitors events and calls function handlers

Response to event may update window or cause other actions

User interacts with computer using mouse or keyboard

Events are generated

Functions known as event handlers are called to run

Event handler function

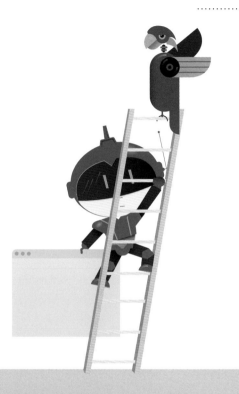

BIG IDEA
GUI STARTS WITH A WINDOW

Any GUI must start with a window that contains everything in the game or application. It holds the icons, graphic images, text, buttons, menus, and so on for the application. The GUI program also should call the main event loop to constantly listen for events.

Creating a Window in Python

To create a window using the Tkinter module, we can use a variable called **window** to hold the information about the window and then give it a title using the following code:

```
window = Tk()
window.title('My First GUI')
```

The final step as mentioned before is to call the main event loop—this must be the LAST line in the code.

```
window.mainloop()
```

Create a new program in a file called GUITest.py to make your first GUI window. Here is the code for this program:

```
from tkinter import *

window = Tk()
window.title('My First GUI')

window.mainloop()   # GUI main event loop
```

You should see a window that looks like any other window on your computer.

SAME CODE, DIFFERENT COMPUTERS

One of the big advantages of the Tkinter module is that the Python code can create a GUI for the computer it is being run on. So if it's on a Windows computer, your GUI window will look similar to other Windows applications. If it's on a Mac, it will looks like a Mac application (the image shown here is from a Mac).

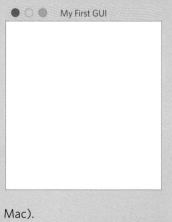

My First GUI

BIG IDEA
CLICKABLE BUTTONS

Now that there is a window, we can add graphical items. Graphical elements such as buttons, labels, menus, and scrollbars are called **widgets**. In this chapter, we will create button, label, entry, and canvas widgets.

For example, we may want to add a Click Me button that, when clicked, prints "Hello, World" to a display area on the screen.

To do this, we need to create two widgets:

❶ A Click Me button widget that, when clicked, causes the action.

❷ A label widget used as a display text area on the screen where the text is shown.

We must also connect the button to the code that will run when the user clicks on it. This code will place information into the display area on the window.

Making Clickable Buttons in Python

For the above example, we will have a Click Me button that, when clicked, prints "Hello, World" to a display area on the screen.

Because we must connect code to the button, we create a function that runs when the button is clicked. Let's call this function **hello_function** and place it before the code to create the widgets.

```
# function called when button is clicked
def hello_function():
    print('Hello, World')  # prints to Shell
    # change display widget to show this text
    display_area.config(text = "Hello, World", \
fg="yellow", bg = "black")
```

ADDING WIDGETS TAKES TWO STEPS

Using a widget such as a button in a GUI program requires two steps:

❶ Creating the widget by calling the Tkinter function and placing it into a variable.

❷ Placing the widget on the screen using Tkinter's layout functions. There are different ways to place these on the screen; in this book, we will use the basic layout method called **pack()**. Other more complex layout methods allow for more control over the appearance and placement of the widgets.

Now, we can add code to create the widgets and then place them on the screen.

```python
# adding a button widget
button1 = Button(window, text="Click Me", command = hello_function)
button1.pack()  # this actually places the button on the window

# adding the display area - using the label widget
display_area = Label(window, text ="")
display_area.pack()  # this actually places the text area on the
window
```

Here is the complete code. Enter it into a file called FirstGUI.py and run it.

```python
# my first GUI program
from tkinter import *

window = Tk()
window.title('My First GUI')

# function to be called when the button is clicked
def hello_function():
    print('Hello, World')  # prints Hello World to the Python Shell
    # change the display Area widget to show this text
    display_area.config(text = "Hello, World", fg="yellow", bg = \
"black")

# adding a button widget
button1 = Button(window, text="Click Me", command = hello_function)
button1.pack()  # this actually places the button on the window

# adding the display area - using the label widget
display_area = Label(window, text ="")
display_area.pack()  # this places text area on window

window.mainloop()  # last line is the GUI main event loop
```

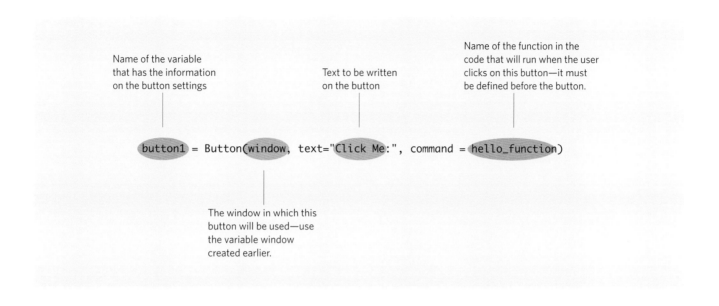

Name of the variable that has the information on the button settings

Text to be written on the button

Name of the function in the code that will run when the user clicks on this button—it must be defined before the button.

```
button1 = Button(window, text="Click Me:", command = hello_function)
```

The window in which this button will be used—use the variable window created earlier.

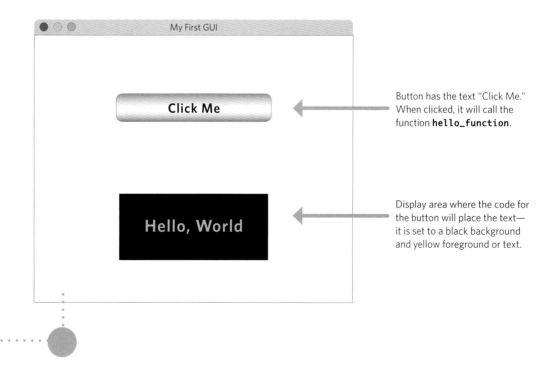

My First GUI

Click Me

Button has the text "Click Me." When clicked, it will call the function **hello_function**.

Hello, World

Display area where the code for the button will place the text— it is set to a black background and yellow foreground or text.

ADDING SHAPES, TEXT, AND IMAGE OBJECTS ON THE SCREEN

For most applications, we need much more than buttons. For example, a game needs objects such as shapes, text, or images on the screen. To hold these objects, we need to create a canvas object that can take in other objects.

How to Display Objects on the Screen in Python

To create a canvas, we create a Canvas widget inside the window, and we specify the width and height. Like we did for the button widget, we create a variable for this widget and then use **pack()** to display it on the screen.

```python
# create a canvas to put objects on the screen
canvas = Canvas(window, width=400,height=400)
canvas.pack()
```

Add the above to the FirstGUI.py file before the final GUI main event loop line, and run it. You should get a blank open canvas area.

Add the following code just after this canvas creation code to create a circle, a rectangle, text, and an image on this canvas. The comments explain the various parameters, including x, y, and color, that must be specified to create each object.

```python
# this creates a red circle at position 100,200, of size 30 by 30
circle = canvas.create_oval(100,200,130,230, fill = 'red')

# creates a blue rectangle with top left at 50,50, of size 20 by 30
blue_rect = canvas.create_rectangle(50,50,70,80, fill = 'blue')

# creates text 'Welcome' in black,font Helvetica 30 at position 200,200
screen_message = canvas.create_text(200,200, text= 'Welcome', \
fill='black', font = ('Helvetica', 30))

# create an image object using the gif file
img = PhotoImage(file="greenChar.gif")
# use image object to create a canvas image at position 100,100
mychar = canvas.create_image(100,100,image = img)
```

Run the file. You should get a red circle, a blue rectangle, "Welcome" text, and a green character image on the screen. See the note on the left to find out where to get and place the green character image.

USING IMAGES IN YOUR CODE: WHERE IS THAT GREEN CHAR?

Before you do your test run, an image named *greenChar.gif* must be in the same folder as the Python file. You can create a small gif file using any drawing tool or download the greenChar.gif file at the website listed on page 138. Make sure the file is not very large and you are using the exact name; the case matters.

MOVING OBJECTS BASED ON KEYBOARD CONTROLS

Now that we have objects, we want to control them in different ways. For example, we may want to move an object when the user clicks on the arrow keys.

Just like we did for the button, we need to create a function to run when a key is pressed, and we must associate or connect (**bind**) this function so that it handles the keyboard inputs. Because each keyboard input is considered an event, these functions are called **event handlers**. The association of this function to the object is called a **binding**. We use a canvas bind function to make this association, or binding, between the event handler function and the keyboard.

Using Keyboard Controls in Python

We must create a function that will handle the keyboard inputs and connect or associate (bind) it to the canvas.

For example, let's say the red circle moves to the right and left with direction from the arrow keys. We can create a function called `move_circle` that decides what key has been pressed and then changes the *x* and *y* amounts in the circle to move it.

To move to the right, we need to change *x* by a positive amount; to move to the left, we move the *x* position by a negative amount.

Here is the code for this function. Add this after the `hello_function` code in the FirstGUI.py file.

```
# move circle to left or right based on keys
def move_circle(event):
    key = event.keysym
    if key == "Right":
        canvas.move(circle,10,0)   # change x
    elif key == "Left":
        canvas.move(circle,-10,0)  # change x
```

Now, we connect or bind this `move_circle` function to the keys using a canvas bind function as follows.

```
# bind keyboard input to move_circle
canvas.bind_all('<Key>', move_circle)
```

Add this canvas bind code just before the final GUI main loop. Run the FirstGui.py file and see if the circle moves with the arrow keys.

MOVING OBJECTS BASED ON MOUSE CLICKS

Sometimes, we want to move or change an object based on the mouse click on the object. We must connect a function that handles the mouse click in a way similar to the event handler for keyboard controls on the last page.

For example, if we want the character to move to where the user clicks on the screen, we must find the *x* and *y* position of the mouse click and update the character to that position. We do this by creating a function that reads the mouse position and updates the character's position, and we bind this function to the mouse click event.

Using Mouse Clicks in Python

Code to move character "mychar" to a new mouse position is done through a function called **move_character** as follows:

```
# function that handles mouse clicks on the character mychar
def move_character(event):
    canvas.coords(mychar,event.x,event.y)
```

Code to bind the character to the mouse clicks is done using a canvas binding as follows:

```
# bind left button mouse to moving the character
canvas.bind_all('<Button-1>', move_character)
```

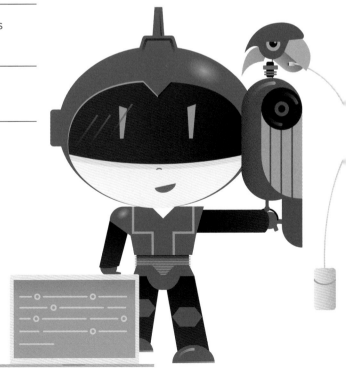

GETTING DATA FROM THE USER

In addition to the use of buttons, mouse, and keyboard input, a GUI program may need to get information typed in by the user using an entry widget. This entry data from the user can then be accessed and processed in the program.

Getting User Data in Python

To get data from the user, an entry widget must be created as follows:

```
user_data = Entry(window,text='')  # initial entry is blank
user_data.pack()
```

To access this data in the rest of the program, use **user_data.get()**.

For example, here is a short program that takes a user entry of a distance in inches, and if it is not empty, converts it to cm and displays the distance when the user clicks on the Convert button.

```
# A unit converter app - from inch to cm

from tkinter import *

def convert():
    if inch_data.get() != "":
        cm_string = str(int(inch_data.get()) * 2.54)
        cm_display.configure(text = cm_string)

window = Tk()
window.title('Inch to cm Converter')

inch_data = Entry(window, text="")
inch_data.pack()

cm_display = Label(window, text="")
cm_display.pack()

button = Button(window, text='Convert to cm', command = convert)
button.pack()

window.mainloop()  # last line is the GUI main event loop
```

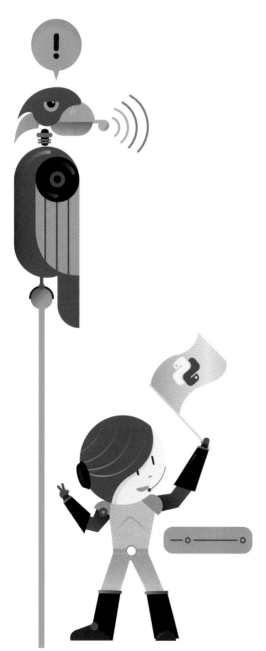

BIG IDEA
GUI CAN SCHEDULE CODE TO RUN

In some projects—games, for example—we need some actions to occur in a loop (i.e., the character moves, enemies appear, etc.) but we also want the screen to be updated and events such as mouse clicks handled. If the GUI mainloop is the last line of code, it will be running continuously, not giving us a chance to run any other code. In order to allow other actions to run in a loop, in addition to the main GUI event loop, we can schedule them with the GUI module.

Scheduling Code to Run with GUI in Python

Before the call to the mainloop, schedule any other actions using the after function. For example:

```python
window.after(100, move_candy)
```

This schedules the **move_candy** function to run after 100 milliseconds. In the function **move_candy**, schedule **move_candy** to run again; this creates a loop and keeps it running during the program. We will see more on how to use this idea in this chapter's project.

EXITING A GUI PROGRAM

....

Because a GUI program uses a loop (mainloop) that runs continuously, updating the screen and handling events, it can end if the user clicks on the window Close button or the program calls a window destroy function.

Exiting GUI in Python

We can add an Exit button that can be clicked to exit the program. We will need a function and to connect it to a button as follows.

```
# function to be called when the button Exit is clicked
def exit_program():
    window.destroy()

qbutton = Button(window, text="Exit", command = exit_program)
qbutton.pack()  # this actually places the button on the window
```

CREATING YOUR OWN ARCADE-STYLE GAME

Let's make a classic arcade-style game with the GUI concepts in this chapter. We will make The Candy Monster Game with the following features:

- The player controls a monster character using arrow keys.
- Candy of different colors appear at random start positions on top and falls to the bottom.
- The player must catch the candy that falls and the score updates to show how many pieces have been caught. If a red (or other bad color) piece of candy is caught, the game ends.
- As the score increases, the candy falls faster and the games gets more difficult.

Obviously, you can change any aspect of the game—the character, the object that falls, the scoring method, and so on.

ARCADE-STYLE GAMES

Arcade-style games are a type of action game similar to the classic coin-operated arcade games. Most of them have simple presentation and gameplay. They involve very little puzzle solving and rely on a player's skill in moving accurately, making quick decisions, and hand-eye coordination. Games usually get more difficult as the play advances.

USING IMAGES IN YOUR GAME WITH GIF FILES

The player character is created using a file of image format GIF (ends in gif). This file should be placed in the same folder as the Python file. The size of the file should not be very large (in the examples provided, they are just 4KB). You can download the sample gif file for this game, greenChar.gif, at the website on page 138 or find another file that is copyright free for your use. You can also create your own character using any bitmap editor. Please note the example in this chapter use gif files because they are the simplest to use in Tkinter. Make sure the file type is gif.

In Tkinter, to use any image on the canvas or in buttons, for example, you must first create an object of type PhotoImage and then use it in the widgets.

Step 1: Create the Initial Game Setup

Here is the pseudocode for this step.

Pseudocode

Import Tkinter and random modules
Create window, and canvas object
Create game title and instructions text object
Set variable score to 0
Create score_display widget to show score
Set level to 1
Create level_display widget to show level
Create character by using an image file
Call the GUI main event loop as the last line of code

Here is the Python code to do the above pseudocode; comments explain each part. Enter the following code into a new file called GUIGame.py.

```
# The Candy Monster game program
from tkinter import *
import random

# make window
window = Tk()
window.title('The Candy Monster Game')

# create a canvas to put objects on the screen
canvas = Canvas(window, width=400, height=400, bg = 'black')
canvas.pack()

# set up welcome screen with title and directions
title = canvas.create_text(200, 200, text= 'The Candy Monster', \
fill='white', font = ('Helvetica', 30))
directions = canvas.create_text(200, 300, text= 'Collect candy \
but avoid the red ones', fill='white', font = ('Helvetica', 20))

# set up score display using label widget
score = 0
score_display = Label(window, text="Score :" + str(score))
score_display.pack()

# set up level display using label widget
level = 1
level_display = Label(window, text="Level :" + str(level))
level_display.pack()

# create an image object using the gif file
player_image = PhotoImage(file="greenChar.gif")
# use image object to create a character at position 200, 360
mychar = canvas.create_image(200, 360, image = player_image)

window.mainloop()  # last line is the GUI main event loop
```

When you run the code at this step, a basic game window with instructions,
similar to the one shown, should appear.

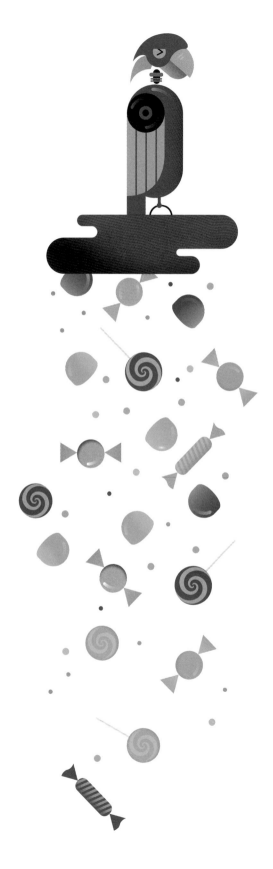

Step 2:
Add Code to Make the Candy and Drop It

Here is the pseudocode for this step.

Pseudocode

- Set candy_list, bad candy_list as empty lists
- Set candy_speed to 2
- Set list for candy colors.
- Define function make_candy()
    - Set x to random position
    - Set y to 0
    - Set c to random color
    - Create canvas oval with x, y, c
    - Add oval to candy_list
    - If color is red, add to bad candy_list
    - Schedules make_candy again
- Define function move_candy()
    - while there is candy in candy_list
        - Increase y
        - If y > edge of screen,
            - Set y to 0, x to random position
    - Schedules move_candy again

Here is the code for this step. Add this to GUIGame.py before the final GUI main event loop and test it. Because we have not yet scheduled the **make_candy** and **move_candy** functions, nothing will change from the first step.

```python
# variables and lists needed for managing candy
candy_list = []  # list containing all candy created, empty at start
bad_candy_list = []  # list containing all bad candy created, empty at start
candy_speed = 2  # initial speed of falling candy
candy_color_list = ['red', 'yellow', 'blue', 'green', 'purple', 'pink', \
'white']

# function to make candy at random places
def make_candy():
    # pick a random x position
    xposition = random.randint(1, 400)
    # pick a random color
    candy_color = random.choice(candy_color_list)
    # create a candy of size 30 at random position and color
    candy = canvas.create_oval(xposition, 0, xposition+30, 30,  fill = \
candy_color)
    # add candy to list
    candy_list.append(candy)
    # if color of candy is red - add it to bad_candy_list
    if candy_color == 'red' :
        bad_candy_list.append(candy)
    # schedule this function to make candy again
    window.after(1000, make_candy)

# function moves candy downwards, and schedules call to move_candy
def move_candy():
    # loop through list of candy and change y position
    for candy in candy_list:
        canvas.move(candy, 0, candy_speed)
        # check if end of screen - restart at random position
        if canvas.coords(candy)[1] > 400:
            xposition = random.randint(1,400)
            canvas.coords(candy, xposition, 0, xposition+30,30)
    # schedule this function to move candy again
    window.after(50, move_candy)
```

Step 3:
Add Code to Update the Score and End the Game

Here is the pseudocode for this step.

Pseudocode

> Define function update_score_level()
>> Increase score, update display
>> If score > 10
>>> Set level to 2, update display
>>> Increase candy_speed.
>> If score > 20
>>> Set level to 3, update display
>>> Increase candy_speed
> Define function end_game_over()
>> Destroy the window,
> Define function end_title()
>> Destroy title, instructions objects

LOCAL VS. GLOBAL VARIABLES

Any variable that is created inside a function (inside the def) is **local** to the function, which means that only the code within the function can access it. The variable is not available after the function (outside the def) has run. Variables that are created outside the function are called **global variables**. They exist for the entire time the program does. All functions can access them, but cannot modify them unless they are declared global inside the function. Because the variables **score**, `level`, and `candy_speed` must be maintained through the game, they are created as global variables outside the **update_score_level** function. The **update_score_level** function will need to modify **score**, **level**, and `candy_speed` variables, so they are declared as global inside the function. Global variables should be avoided when possible since they can be changed in different and sometimes unexpected places, making it difficult to find problems in a program. We can avoid the use of global variables by using more advanced programming techniques that are beyond the scope of this book.

Here is the code for this step. Add this to the end of the code from the last step, again making sure it is before the last GUI main event loop line. Because these functions have not been scheduled, there is no change from Step 1; the score does not update yet.

```python
# function updates score, level and candy_speed
def update_score_level():
    # use of global since variables are changed
    global score, level, candy_speed
    score = score + 1
    score_display.config(text="Score :" + \
str(score))
    # determine if level needs to change
    # update level and candy speed
    if score > 5 and score <= 10:
        candy_speed = candy_speed + 1
        level = 2
        level_display.config(text="Level :" + \
str(level))
    elif score > 10:
        candy_speed = candy_speed + 1
        level = 3
        level_display.config(text="Level :" + \
str(level))

# function called to end game - destroys window
def end_game_over():
    window.destroy()

# this destroys the instructions on the screen
def end_title():
    canvas.delete(title)  # remove title
    canvas.delete(directions)  # remove directions
```

Step 4:
Add Code to Check If Character and Candy Collide

We now need to add code to determine when the character touches the candy and delete it from the list of candy. If it is a bad candy, we must call an end to the game.

Here is the pseudocode for this step.

Pseudocode

Define function collision(item1, item2, distance)
  Set x to horizontal difference between items
  Set y to vertical difference between items
  Set overlap to x < distance and y < distance
  Return overlap

Define function check_hits()
  While there is item in candy_list
    If item is hit by character
      If item is in badcandy_list
        Set up Game over screen
        Schedule end_game_over
      Else
        Call update_score_level

Here is the code for this step; add this to the file once again before the last GUI main event line. Because these functions are not being called yet, there will be no change detected at this stage.

```
# check distance between 2 objects - return true if they 'touch'
def collision(item1, item2, distance):
    xdistance = abs(canvas.coords(item1)[0] - canvas.coords(item2)[0])
    ydistance = abs(canvas.coords(item1)[1] - canvas.coords(item2)[1])
    overlap = xdistance < distance and ydistance < distance
    return overlap


# checks if character hit bad candy, schedule end_game_over
# if character hits candy, remove from screen, list, update score
def check_hits():
    # check if it hit a bad candy - need to end game
    for candy in bad_candy_list:
        if collision(mychar, candy, 30):
            game_over = canvas.create_text(200, 200, text= 'Game \
Over', fill='red', font = ('Helvetica', 30))
            # end game but after user can see score
            window.after(2000, end_game_over)
            # do not check any other candy, window to be destroyed
            return
    # check if it hit any good candy
    for candy in candy_list:
        if collision(mychar, candy, 30):
            canvas.delete(candy)  # remove from canvas
            # find where in list and remove and update score
            candy_list.remove(candy)
            update_score_level()
    # schedule check Hits again
    window.after(100, check_hits)
```

Step 5:
Add Code to Control the Character with the Arrow Keys

We must now add code to control the player character with the arrow keys. If we call a function each time the arrow key is pressed, the control will not be smooth. Instead, we determine which direction the character should move when the arrow keys are first pressed, we keep track of this move direction in a variable called `move_direction`, and then when the arrow keys are released, we update the variable `move_direction`. Finally, we update the character position based on the `move_direction` value, checking that it does not go off the edge of the screen.

Here is the pseudocode for this step.

Pseudocode

```
Set move_direction to 0
Define function check_input(event)
    If key pressed is right
        Set move_direction to right
    If key pressed is left
        Set move_direction to left
Define function end_input(event)
    Set move_direction to None
Define move_character()
    If move_direction is right AND within screen
    edge
        Increase character x
    If move_direction is left AND within screen edge
        Decrease character x
    Schedule move_character after 16 ms

Set canvas binding key press to check_input
Set canvas binding key release to end_input
```

Here is the code for this step. Add this code to your file again just before the final GUI main event loop line. Because the `move_character` function has not been scheduled, there will again be no change when the program is run.

FRAMES PER SECOND

Frames Per Second (FPS) is an indication of how quickly images are updated on the screen. It refers to how many images (frames) you can see each second. In games, users can expect 60 frames per second. In this game, to provide a smooth movement, we will handle the keyboard input at 60 FPS, which is every 1/60 second (1/60 * 1000 milliseconds = approx. 16 ms). This is the reason the `move_character` function is scheduled every 16 ms. You can experiment with this number and make it higher on slower computers (e.g., 30 frames per second may also be acceptable; that computes to 1/30 = 33 ms).

```
move_direction = 0 # track which direction player is moving
# Function handles when user first presses arrow keys
def check_input(event):
    global move_direction
    key = event.keysym
    if key == "Right":
        move_direction = "Right"
    elif key == "Left":
        move_direction = "Left"

# Function handles when user stop pressing arrow keys
def end_input(event):
    global move_direction
    move_direction = "None"

# Function checks if not on edge and updates x coordinates based on right/left
def move_character():
    if move_direction == "Right" and canvas.coords(mychar)[0] < 400:
        canvas.move(mychar, 10,0)
    if move_direction == "Left" and canvas.coords(mychar)[0] > 0 :
        canvas.move(mychar, -10,0)
    window.after(16, move_character)  # Move character at 60 frames per second

# bind the keys to the character
canvas.bind_all('<KeyPress>', check_input)  # bind key press
canvas.bind_all('<KeyRelease>', end_input)  # bind all keys to circle
```

Step 6:
Start the Game!

Schedule End of Instructions and Functions to Make Candy, Move Candy, Check Hits, Move Character, and Start the Game Loop

Schedule a call to destroy the title and starting instructions and then schedule a call to all the functions needed to run the game (**make_candy**, **move_candy**, **check_hits**, and **move_character**). Finally, make sure the main game loop is still the last line of code, so all events are handled.

Here is the additional code for this step. Make sure it is added before the final GUI main event loop line.

```
# Start game loop by scheduling all the functions
window.after(1000, end_title)  # destroy title and instructions
window.after(1000, make_candy)  # start making candy
window.after(1000, move_candy)  # start moving candy
window.after(1000, check_hits)  # check if character hit a candy
window.after(1000, move_character)  # handle keyboard controls
```

EXPERIMENT AND EXTEND

Experiment 1:
Make a Password Generator

Create an app in which the user clicks on a button to produce a randomly generated password. Create the password by combining common words, separators, and numbers.

Pseudocode

Import Tkinter and random modules
Set up word list and separators list
make_password function
    Get random word from word list
    Add to random item from separator list
Set up GUI window
Set up button with make_password callback

Code Hint

Here is some sample code to combine strings chosen at random from lists.

```
commonWords=['cat', 'dog', 'jump', 'train', \
'toast', 'water', 'phone']
specialChars = ['!', '$', '%']

password = random.choice(commonWords) + random. \
choice(specialChars) + random.choice(commonWords) \
+ str(random.randint(0,100)) + random. \
choice(specialChars)
```

Experiment 2:
Make a Song Lyrics Generator App

Add a graphic user interface to the song lyrics generator project from Chapter 1. Create an app in which the user answers some questions and clicks on a button to generate a song based on their entries. Add an image on the button using code as follows (where musicNotes.gif is an image in the same folder as the Python file. You can get this image from the website listed on page 138 or make your own image).

```
button_image = PhotoImage(file="musicNotes.gif")

button = Button(window, text = 'Create \
Song',image = button_image, compound = TOP, \
command = create_song)
button.pack()
```

To set a color on the window, you can use:

```
window.configure(bg="MediumPurple1")
```

You can also set the same color in the labels using:

```
red_label = Label(window,text='Enter something red \
, e.g. roses: ',bg="MediumPurple1", fg= 'black',)
```

You may also have to add an empty label to add some space on the top of the app using:

```
top_label = Label(window,text='',bg="MediumPurple1")
top_label.pack()
```

Song Lyrics Generator

Something red, e.g., roses:

robins

Something blue, e.g. violets:

mittens

Something you love, e.g. puppies:

kittens

Verb, e.g., singing:

dancing

Create Song Lyrics

robins are red
mittens are blue
I like kittens
But not as much as I love dancing with you!

Experiment 3:
Make a Voting App

Create an app in which the user clicks on the button of their choice to vote, and the vote count updates. For example, a voting app could find out if the person is a dog lover or a cat lover. The code is similar to the score update in the game project in this chapter.

Voting App

Cat person?

Dog person?

Cat lovers = 2

Dog lovers = 3

Experiment 4:
Create an Arcade-style Survival Game

Make changes and extensions to the Candy Monster game to create a Spider Survival game in which the player must avoid the objects (spiders) instead of catching them. The goal is to survive for as long as possible, and the score field at the bottom indicates how many seconds they have survived. As before, the game gets more difficult by increasing the speed of the objects over time.

Here are some changes that you may need:

A new graphic for the player; for example, you could use the stick figure gif file available at the website listed on page 138 and change the code to use this image.

```
player_image = PhotoImage(file="stickfigure.gif")
mychar = canvas.create_image(200,360,image = \
player_image)
```

Use a spider graphic instead of the canvas objects that were used to make the candy. Place this code outside the **make_spiders** function (which is a version of the **make_candy** function).

```
spider_image = PhotoImage(file="spider.gif")
```

And inside the **make_spiders** function, use the following:

```
    yposition = random.randint(1,400)
    spider = canvas.create_ \
image(0,yposition,image = spider_image)
    # add spider to list
    spider_list.append(spider)
```

Here is the additional code you will need to add so the player can move in all four directions and cannot escape into the edges. In the **check_input**, add the following:

```
if key == "Up":
    move_direction = "Up"
elif key == "Down":
    move_direction = "Down"
```

Change the **move_character** function to use all directions and check edges:

```python
def move_character():
    if move_direction == "Right" and canvas. \
coords(mychar)[0] < 400:
        canvas.move(mychar, 10,0)
    if move_direction == "Left" and canvas. \
coords(mychar)[0] > 0 :
        canvas.move(mychar, -10,0)
    if move_direction == "Up" and canvas. \
coords(mychar)[1] > 0 :
        canvas.move(mychar, 0,-10)
    if move_direction == "Down" and canvas. \
coords(mychar)[1] < 400:
        canvas.move(mychar, 0,10)
    window.after(16, move_character)
```

Change the movement so the spiders appear on the left and move to the right. Note the spiders do not come back once they reach the edge.

```python
# function moves spiders from left to right
def move_spider():
    # loop through list and change x position
    for spider in spider_list:
        canvas.move(spider, spider_speed, 0)
    window.after(50, move_spider)
```

Change the way the score updates, so it updates every second and not when there are hits.

Experiment 5: Two-player Games and More

Once you understand the code to make one of these games, extend the games and/or add other extensions. For example:

- Turn the Spider Survival game into a Road Crossing game, in which you update the score only if player can move across the screen, avoiding spiders and/or other objects, and reach a home icon safely.
- Create a Treasure Hunt game in which the player has to move around collecting treasure and avoiding enemies. When the player reaches a portal icon, the background and objects change to create a new room or level.
- Customize the images and/or add background image to the window by using a canvas image object centered on the canvas.
- Turn any of these games into a two-player game. For example, in the Spider Survival game, create another player using a different image that is controlled by WASD keys. Display scores for both players at the bottom.
- Add a laser or missile launch feature for when you press the Space key. You can create a new canvas object that starts at the player and add it to a new laser list and then schedule a function that moves items in the laser list and checks if it hits other items in the game.

Invite your friends and family to showcase your coding skills and test your apps and games. Get feedback on how to improve your projects further.

WHAT'S NEXT?

Now that you have learned to code several projects in Python, what's next? Here are some ways to use your powerful new skill and expand your knowledge of coding in Python.

Use Python with the micro:bit for Physical Computing: Program LEDs, Motors, Speakers, and More

The **micro:bit** is a small and inexpensive computer (powered by a microcontroller) that can be programmed using MicroPython—a special version of Python for microcontrollers. You can use MicroPython online on microbit.org or download an editor like Mu (codewith.mu). Using Python code, you can control LEDs (light emitting diodes), motors, play music on speakers, and much more.

Here is a simple example of Python code that turns on an LED light, displays a check mark on the display when button A is pressed, and then turns the light off and displays an X when button B is pressed. In addition, if the micro:bit is shaken, it displays a random number from 1 to 6 (acts like a digital dice). You could use a micro:bit project like this to build your own custom game board, for example.

Pressing this Button A turns ON the LED and displays a check

Pressing this Button B turns OFF the LED and displays an X

May need to add a resistor here, depending on the type of LED

LED

+ve (long leg) connected to pin 1

-ve (short leg) connected to GND

```python
from microbit import *
import random
pin1.write_digital(0)  # light is off
display.show(Image.NO)
while True: # repeat forever
  if accelerometer.was_gesture("shake"):
    roll = random.randint(1,6)
    display.show(str(roll))  # show random number
  elif button_a.is_pressed():
    display.show(Image.YES)
    pin1.write_digital(1)  # turn  light on
  elif button_b.is_pressed():
    display.show(Image.NO)
    pin1.write_digital(0)  # turn light off
```

Use Python on the Raspberry Pi

The **Raspberry Pi** is a small and inexpensive general-purpose computer that comes with Python 3 installed. In addition to running all the Python projects in this book on the Raspberry Pi, you can use it for physical computing by connecting the row of GPIO (general-purpose input/output) pins to LEDs, motors, speakers, and more. Or, you can extend the Raspberry Pi using an add-on board like the Sense Hat. Here is a simple example of using Python to control an LED and a button connected to the Raspberry Pi.

```
from gpiozero import LED, Button
led = LED(17)
button = Button(2)
while True:
  if button.is_pressed:
    led.on()
  else:
    led.off()
```

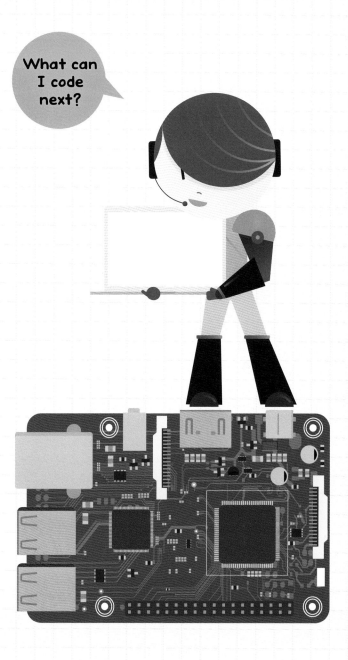

PHYSICAL COMPUTING AND THE MAKER MOVEMENT

The micro:bit and the Raspberry Pi are popular in the maker movement, a trend where anyone can use their creativity and building skills to create objects from different materials. Using code, a maker can make fun and/or useful items that come alive with spinning motors, blinking lights, and more.

Expand Your Knowledge of Python with These Additional Concepts

In addition to learning more ways to use the concepts covered in this book—lists, conditionals, loops, and so on—you can expand your knowledge of Python with some concepts that aren't covered in this book. Here are a few to look at next.

Dictionaries

These are lists that are not ordered and each item is a **key-value pair**. This can be useful in many projects. Here is a simple example of using a dictionary called **scores** to keep track of scores of different players. The key is the name of the player and the value is the score. This is much easier than using multiple variables or a list.

```
scores = {'Mia': 56, 'Nico': 44, 'Joe': 97, 'Ana' : 100}
print(scores['Ana'])  # this prints 100, value for key Ana
```

Exception Handling

We did some basic error checking in the projects in this book—for example, in the Chapter 4 dice game project, we checked to make sure the user entered the correct number of choices. However, there are many other errors that can occur when a project runs. Errors that are detected when the program runs are called **exceptions**. To make a robust program, we want to exit the program gracefully with an error message in all cases. In order to do that, we will have to check for several possibilities: for example, is the file to be opened available, is the number entered valid, and so on. Python provides an easy way to do exception handling with the try/except statement. Here is a very simple example where we recover from any error due to an invalid number entry or a divide by 0.

```
try:
    candy = input('Enter amount of candy ')
    persons = input('Enter number of people ')
    print('Candy per person is', int(candy) // int(persons))
except:
    print('Error. Unable to calculate candy amount')
```

files

dictionaries

exception handling

physical computing

Files

Your project may need to save and read information to a computer file to be used next time it is run (for example the high score of the player). Python has many ways to create, read, and modify different kinds of files. Here is a very simple example that opens a file containing high scores and prints out the information.

```
fhandle = open('highscores.txt', 'r')  # opens file for reading
scores = fhandle.read()  # gets all content from file
print(scores)
fhandle.close()
```

Extend Your Python Powers by Using Other Standard Python Modules

There are several modules in the Python Standard Library and are part of the Python download. We have already used the following in this book:

■ Chapter 2: **Turtle** module, to do turtle graphics
■ Chapter 3: **Time** module, to create a pause in the adventure game
■ Chapter 4: **Random** module, to get a random number for a roll for the dice
■ Chapter 5: **Tkinter** module, to create GUI games and apps

These standard modules are a good start. You can extend your skills with these additional modules that are also part of the Python Standard Library:

■ **Math** gives access to math functions like pi or square root.
■ **Statistics** allows use of functions like mean, median, and variance.
■ **Datetime** makes operations on time and date easy.
■ **CSV** handles files in Comma Separated Values format, which is commonly used in spreadsheets and databases.
■ **Webbrowser** allows you to display Web documents to users.

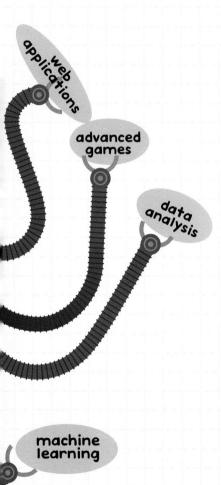

web applications

advanced games

data analysis

machine learning

Master Programming Tools to Make Coding Easier

While using IDLE, you must have noticed how it helps you write Python programs by indenting code as needed, color coding different parts of Python, and highlighting syntax errors. Here are some other tools in IDLE that can make programming even easier.

Debugger

For most of the projects in this book, if you add a small amount of code at every step as suggested, and then test each step before going to the next, you probably won't come across errors that are too difficult to find or fix. However, to make coding easier, especially on larger projects, you should learn to use a debugger. A **debugger** is a tool that helps test and find bugs in your code in many ways. For example, it lets you run the code one line at a time, stop the code running when it reaches a certain line, and displays the value of the variables in the program at any point. IDLE has a debugger built in, which you can find in Python Shell by clicking on Debug On.

Code Completion with Autocomplete

With the **autocomplete** feature in IDLE, you do not need to remember the exact name and usage of the functions, and you can discover new functions as you code. This assisted intelligent code completion makes coding much easier. To use autocomplete in IDLE, enter the name of the variable and the '.' and wait for IDLE to prompt with all the possible functions. See the screenshot showing all possible functions to be used on the string 's'. Once you select the function and enter the first '(', IDLE prompts with the list of parameters needed for the function.

In addition to using autocomplete, you can also use the Python **dir** function to find all possible functions. For example, if you have a string **s**, type in **dir(s)** in the Python Shell to list all the ways you can manipulate the string.

IDLE is an example of an IDE (Integrated Development Environment) that is free with the Python download. You can use other IDEs and editors like **PyCharm** from JetBrains or Microsoft's **Visual Studio Code** that offer more powerful tools for debugging and intelligent code completion.

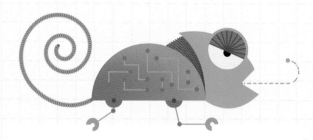

```
>>> s = 'hello'
>>> s.
    capitalize
    casefold
    center
    count
    encode
    endswith
    expandtabs
    find
    format
    format_map
```

```
>>> s = 'hello'
>>> dir(s)
['__add__', '__class__', '__contains__', '__delattr__', '__dir__', '__doc__',
'__eq__', '__format__', '__ge__', '__getattribute__', '__getitem__', '__getnewargs__',
'__gt__', '__hash__', '__init__', '__init_subclass__', '__iter__', '__le__',
'__len__', '__lt__', '__mod__', '__mul__', '__ne__', '__new__', '__reduce__',
'__reduce_ex__', '__repr__', '__rmod__', '__rmul__', '__setattr__', '__sizeof__',
'__str__', '__subclasshook__', 'capitalize', 'casefold', 'center', 'count', 'encode',
'endswith', 'expandtabs', 'find', 'format', 'format_map', 'index', 'isalnum',
'isalpha', 'isascii', 'isdecimal', 'isdigit', 'isidentifier', 'islower', 'isnumeric',
'isprintable', 'isspace', 'istitle', 'isupper', 'join', 'ljust', 'lower', 'lstrip',
'maketrans', 'partition', 'replace', 'rfind', 'rindex', 'rjust', 'rpartition',
'rsplit', 'rstrip', 'split', 'splitlines', 'startswith', 'strip', 'swapcase',
'title', 'translate', 'upper', 'zfill']
>>> s.capitalize()
'Hello'
>>>
```

Go Even Further by Using Powerful Third-Party Python Packages

Since Python is a popular and open source language, there is an active community of users and contributors who have created software for a variety of applications. They make their software available for free as packages (collections of modules) for other Python developers. You can check what is available at the Python Package Index at pypi.org. Here is a small list of some popular third-party Python packages that you can look at next.

- **PyGame** (Pygame.org) allows you to build 2-D games in Python.
- Use Python code to build and control **Minecraft Pi**, a special edition of Minecraft made for Raspberry Pi.
- **Requests** (docs.python-requests.org/en/master) and **BeautifulSoup** (crummy.com/software/BeautifulSoup) packages help you access content on the Internet in your projects.
- **Kivy** (kivy.org) allows you to create multi-touch Python apps across multiple platforms.
- **Matplotlib** (matplotlib.org) is a popular package for data analysis.
- **Scikit-learn** (scikit-learn.org) offers easy to use tools for machine learning in Python.

Learn How to Get Help

As you do more coding projects on your own, you may have questions. There are many ways to get help:

- **Built-in offline Help pages.** When on the Python shell, click on Help, then click on Python Docs, and you will be able to access the offline Help pages for Python. You can either enter a search term in the search box or read the tutorial or Python documentation.
- **Ask other programmers.** Search on the Internet to see if someone else posted the same question. A popular site used by programmers to ask questions and share solutions is Stack Overflow (stackoverflow.com).
- **Search using Google with Python as your first word.** Example: "python turtle circle" will provides links to the Python.org documentation and tips on other tutorials or answers by other Python programmers (often on Stack Overflow).
- **Visit Python.org,** which is a good starting point to find other Python resources.

Expand Your Coding Skills by Learning Object-Oriented Programming

When you write larger projects and/or work with others, you will find it easier to divide and manage your work using a different way of programming called **object-oriented programming**. Instead of focusing on the functions and order of running the program, this approach looks at the project as different objects, where each object contains both how the data is stored and how it is manipulated. Object-oriented programming is done in Python using classes.

Get Inspired! Check Out How Other Programmers Are Using Python

Python is used successfully in many applications across the world. Here are a few examples. See more under success stories on Python.org.

- **3-D models and 3-D animation.** Python integrates with **Blender** (blender.org), a free and open 3-D animation tool. Artists and animators use Python to automate tasks and build models and animations in Blender that would not be possible without code.
- **Web applications.** Many parts of the Internet—including **Google**, **YouTube**, and **Twitter**—use Python in some way. Python programmers continue to build Web applications using Python since it is fast, secure, scalable, and easy to use because of access to many powerful Python frameworks like **Django** and **Flask**.
- **Scientific research.** Several scientists use Python to analyze data in their research because of data science packages like **NumPy** and **Matplotlib**. There are also Python libraries available that can handle specific kinds of scientific data; for example, the **Biopython Project** provides Python tools for computational molecular biology.
- **Artificial intelligence and machine learning.** Python programmers are building intelligent applications that use machine learning to recognize faces, understand speech, detect objects, recommend products, find fraud, and much more. Python provides access to several powerful machine learning libraries and packages like **TensorFlow** and **scikit-learn**.
- **Creating Music.** Python can be used in music projects in different ways. For example, **FoxDot** provides a rich environment to create music.

The only way to learn to code is to spend a lot of time coding. Work through all the small code examples under the Big Idea sections to understand the fundamental ideas in programming, build your own version of the chapter projects, and then strengthen your understanding by trying out all the Experiment and Extend projects. Building your own projects using your creativity and Python code is not only a good way to learn to code, but is also a lot of fun.

GLOSSARY

Algorithm: A set of steps listed in order to do a task—for example, the recipe to make a cake or the steps to find the average of a list of scores

Autocomplete: Automatically shows all the possible ways to complete the code—for example, the possible functions for a string. IDLE, and other IDEs have auto-complete to make coding easier

Binding: Connecting a function that will be run for an event or an object—for example, binding the function that moves a character when a key is pressed to the keyboard object

Boolean: A statement that is either true or false—for example, 5 > 3 is true but 3 > 5 is false

Bugs: Mistakes in the code that cause the program to run differently than expected

Canvas: Part of the application window used to display shapes, images, etc.

Chatbot: A program that talks to humans using text

Code: Set of instructions in a language the computer understands to do a particular task

Comments: Notes for the programmer to make the code easier to understand and change later—in Python, these are entered by adding a # before them.

Condition: A Boolean expression that evaluates to true or false—for example, score > 100 can be true or false depending on the value of the score at that point in the game

Conditional: Statement that is run based on something being true and false—if then else statements are conditionals.

Conditional loop: A set of instructions that repeat so long as a condition is true—for example, while score < 10 is a conditional loop that runs the block of code that follows till the score is less than 10

Data: Information stored by the computer

Debugger: A tool that helps in testing and finding bugs in a program

Debugging: Finding and removing a bug or mistake in the code

Event-driven programming: Where the program or code runs based on an event (an action by a user or some other program)

Event handler: A piece of code that runs when an event is triggered—for example, a function that displays "Hello" when a button is clicked is the event handler for the button click event

Exceptions: Errors that can occur when a program is running that can cause it to stop

Floats: Decimal numbers like 4.23 are called floats.

Flowcharts: A visual way of showing an algorithm

Function: This is code that has a name and does something and in some cases, takes in information. Python has standard functions like print, input, etc.

FPS: Frames per second, an indication of how fast the screen updates per second

GIF: A file format for images, used in the Chapter 5 examples in this book

GUI: Graphical user interfaces allow a user to interact with the computer using graphical elements like icons and not just using text.

Global variables: Variables that can be accessed by all parts of the program

Imports: A way to give access to the functions and definitions in a module in Python

Integers: Whole numbers like 43 are known as integers.

IDE: Short for integrated development environment, IDE is an application that allows users to enter and edit code as well as run it. It provides tools to make coding easier. An example of IDE is IDLE.

Interpreter: Reads code written by user and runs it on the machine

Local variables: Variables that can be changed or used only within a function

Loops: A repeating a set of instructions

Module: A file in Python that has functions and definitions—for example, turtle module has functions to use the Python turtle

Nested conditional: A conditional statement inside another conditional sentence

Nested loop: A loop inside another loop

Object-oriented programming: A way of coding where the program is organized as objects with data and functions that can manipulate the object

Parameters: Information given to a function—for example, the print function takes the string to be printed as a parameter

Physical computing: Programming objects in the world like LEDs, motors, speakers, and more

Program: A set of instructions to do a task in a language the computer understands

Pseudocode: Algorithm written in an informal natural language like English

Random: Something that has an element of chance, changes each time, or is not fixed

Runtime error: A mistake that appears when the program is run

Shell: An interactive part of Python IDLE where you can enter Python code for experimenting; also a place where text is entered to a program, or output of a program is displayed

Strings: Any text is known as a string and is entered with a single or double quote. 'Hello' and "Susan" are strings.

Syntax error: A mistake in the usage of the programming language—for example, a wrong spelling

Value: Content of the variable

Variables: Item that stores information—it has a name and a value and corresponds to location in memory.

Widgets: Graphical elements like buttons, labels, menus that are part of a GUI program

Window: Part of the GUI program, the window is a separate viewing area on the computer screen corresponding to an application.

RESOURCES

Python

Download Python for free, get help with Python problems and questions, and learn more about programming.

www.python.org

Creative Coding in Python

Your source for all things related to this book.

www.creativecodinginpython.com

Quarto Knows

View and download the complete code for all of the projects in this book, as well as images used in the projects, from the publisher's website.

www.quartoknows.com/page/creativecoding

Computers for Creativity

More information on programing (in Python and other languages) and its uses, plus project ideas and resources for teachers. The author's website.

www.computersforcreativity.com

ACKNOWLEDGMENTS

Thank you to my husband and best friend, Vijay, for encouraging me to write this book and supporting me at every step. Thanks to my daughter Trisha and my son Kyle for giving their honest feedback on what is "cool" and fun, and helping me transition from a computer programmer to teaching middle school kids. Without them, I would never have been able to design projects for my classes or for this book. Special thanks to Kyle for his video game expertise. My gratitude to my mother for teaching me the joy of hard work, and for the wonderful meals over my summer writing months. Thank you to my friends and extended family for your warm reception to my book project and your valuable technical advice.

I am grateful to my years of teaching experience at the Los Altos School District and the innovative administrators, Jeff, Alyssa, Sandra, and Karen, who supported me in the best job ever—bringing computer science to every student in the district. I would like to acknowledge the teacher community—the STEM team at LASD, the hundreds of teachers who took my coding workshops at KCI Foothill college, and the amazing #csk8 and CSTA (Computer Science Teachers Association) groups. Your enthusiastic reception of my lessons made me believe that I should share my teaching methods through a book.

And finally, and most importantly, thanks to the many hundreds of students who have learned to code in my classes over the years. Your excitement to learn and your creative projects inspired me to write this book.

ABOUT THE AUTHOR

....

Sheena Vaidyanathan teaches a Python-based computer science class to 11–13 year olds and is the computer science integration specialist in the Los Altos School District, in Los Altos, California, where she has also designed computer science curricula, conducted professional development for the K–8 STEM program, and taught pre-algebra, digital design, and visual art. She is also the program director for the computer science professional development programs at Krause Center for Innovation, Foothill College, where she teaches teachers to code in Python, Scratch, and other languages. Over the years, hundreds of students and teachers have learned to code in her classes. She shares her many years of experience teaching coding by writing articles, presenting at conferences, and providing best practices and student work on her personal website, **computersforcreativity.com**. Prior to teaching, Vaidyanathan worked in Silicon Valley for more than 10 years as a computer scientist and technology entrepreneur. She lives in Los Altos, California.

INDEX